Being Salt

Being Salt

A Theology of an Ordered Church

George R. Sumner

BEING SALT
A Theology of an Ordered Church

ISBN 13: 978-1-55635-091-7

Cataloging-in-Publication data:

Being salt : a theology of an ordered church / George R. Sumner.

x + 110 p.; 20 cm.

ISBN 13: 978-1-55635-091-7

1. Ordination. 2. Ordination—Anglican Communion. 3. Pastoral Theology. I. Title

BV660 .S89 2007

Manufactured in the U.S.A.

This book is dedicated to the beloved community of Wycliffe College, Toronto, where we strive by God's grace to prepare, among other future leaders, evangelical Anglican clergy who are salt for the earth.

". . . but let them know which put their hands unto this plough, that once consecrated unto God they are made his peculiar inheritance forever."

Richard Hooker
Laws of Ecclesiastical Polity, Book V

Contents

Acknowledgements ix

Introduction 1

1. The Priest as Counter-Symbol 21

2. The Priest as the Sign of the Oath 45

3. The Priest as Church in Miniature 61

4. So What? 77

Bibliography 105

Scripture Index 109

Acknowledgements

The first section of chapter 1 was presented as a paper for the Scholar-Pastor program of the Center for Theological Inquiry, 1999. The main idea of chapter 3 was used in a retreat for Little Trinity parish, Toronto, in the spring of 2002, and for a renewal conference, "Christ our Life," in Burlington, in the fall. A section of chapter 4 has been reworked from my inaugural speech as Principal of Wycliffe College in 1999. The work as a whole has been presented to clergy conferences in the Dioceses of Saskatchewan, Fredericton, and Rio Grande. I am grateful for insightful comments from Dr. Joe Mangina of Wycliffe, the Rev. Dr. Leander Harding of Trinity, Ambridge, and Dr. Jeremy Begbie of St. Andrews. Richard and Cinda Clark were helpful in the editing process; I am grateful to Wipf and Stock for their confidence in the value of this unusual subject.

Introduction

THIS ESSAY AIMS TO provide a convincing answer to a single question: why ordination for life? One can readily think of a number of reasons not to bother asking it. Surely in a Church environment troubled with ethics scandals, declining membership, global epidemic, and doctrinal battles, Church folk already have enough to handle. Why a question so seemingly minor and technical? Why not leave well enough alone?

The truth is that the question is raised on the contemporary Church scene repeatedly, if only implicitly. Anglicans ink concordats with Lutheran neighbors, some of whom have, until now, had neither bishops-for-life nor a diaconate in the same three-fold, traditional sense as their Anglican brothers and sisters. Older ecumenical arrangements, like the pioneering one in South India, included Presbyterians who often understand a pastor's call to last as long as his or (now) her service in a congregation. Throughout rural dioceses in North America there is a wave of interest in "total ministry," with its emphasis on the ministry of the laity. According to this trend of thought, ordained ministry needs to be taken down a peg, and to be thought of in a thoroughly functional way.[1] Even if an alternative has not yet been proposed, the logic of such an approach moves inexorably in a direction away from the life-long priest. Finally, the strongly evangelical Anglican diocese of Sydney, Australia emits rumblings about initiating lay presidency at the Eucharist. In a variety of ways, the nature and prerogatives of the priest are called into question. One aspect of this interrogation about the nature of priesthood is the question of duration.

Behind these recent stirrings are deeper cultural assumptions that militate against lifelong orders. The democratic impulse is repelled by any whiff of clerical privilege, and contemporary practicality moves naturally in the direction of pastors employed because they have distinct gifts utilized in the most suitable place. It may be that a particular person has the requisite skills to remain in pastoral work, in various settings, until retirement, but it needn't be so. If the economy at large is moving toward shorter, multiple careers, why should we be surprised if the clergy follow suit? Finally, if one adds a general sense of resistance to traditional claims to authority, one should not be surprised at the high levels of clergy discouragement and "burn-out" in the face of their diminished lot.

1. See Josephine Borgeson and Lynne Wilson, eds., *Reshaping Ministry: Essays in Memory of Wesley Frensdorff* (Arvada: Jethro, 1990) including the essay on local ordination among Navajo people by the present author.

The beginning of this essay's composition was simultaneous with the volcanic eruption of scandal related to priestly abuse in the Roman Catholic Church in the United States. So, one might offer a moral objection to indelibility, as well, namely that a renewed emphasis on the lifelong nature of ordination wrongfully gives comfort to abusers, who might grasp hold of their priestly identity regardless of their conduct. In fairness, the tradition has never in any way suggested that abusive priests should nonetheless carry on with their work because of the indelible nature of their priesthood. Still, some might mishear the message, given the moment. It will be morally incumbent on an argument for the continued practice of the lifelong priesthood to show how it is not prey to such misuse.

The truth is that ordinands in seminaries, even the brightest and most devout, have an implicit problem with the concept of priesthood for life. They insist that they want to promote the ministries of God's people. They observe that religious communities need guidance. They feel themselves to have a gift in focusing the worshipping Eucharistic community. They may even feel they are good at being rather than doing, and so will provide a salve for a frenetic people. But none of this escapes the critique of the useful and functional, and so all of it might be best accomplished, Presbyterian-style, for as long as energy or capacity endures. When all this runs its skein, why, still, a priest for life?[2]

2. The importance of the question finds an ally in a most unlikely corner, with a very different method, namely a Jungian approach to

If the question seems far-fetched, one may compare a conversation I once had as a missionary in east Africa. My wife and I were staying at the Franciscan friary in Dar es Salaam, Tanzania, where we heard of the difficulty Anglican religious have in recruiting East Africans, especially because of the demand for life-long celibacy. The Franciscans were wondering if a different model might be necessary for their context, maybe a "term-limited" service for younger men (much as the Buddhists in Thailand practice). But what would this do to the very meaning of being a Franciscan? The analogy to the issue of life-long priesthood is readily apparent.

To be clear, we are not claiming that this question is in fact being asked much, either by ordinands, clergy, or their parishioners. But we are claiming that there is a certain incoherence in our understanding of ministry which is exposed when one does ask it. The muddle ministry is in has an unwitting relationship to the question of the real nature of orders. That question in turn has a direct bearing on the questions the ordained or about-to-be-ordained do ask, namely "what is a priest anyway?" and so "what am I supposed to be doing?" If your parish has conflict between the expectations of council and collared, or has a pastor trapped agoraphobically in front of his computer, or has a young priest with a burgeoning shelf of books on corporate

---

theology. For the indelible mark is the archetype of which priesthood would be the expression. On this see William Perri, *A Radical Challenge for Priesthood Today: From Trial to Transformation* (Mystic, CT: Twenty-third Publications, 1996).

leadership self-help, then this question stalks your Church life unasked.

Buried amidst these worries of seminarian and religious is a profoundly theological concern, one that lies at the center of this essay as well. Potential priests worth their salt know that any gifts they do have for ministry are solely gifts of grace. He or she did nothing to create them, though they are called to acknowledge gifts given. But if this is so, isn't the very notion of a lifelong, irrevocable endowment moving in the very opposite direction? Won't it convey a sense, not of grace, but of possession? So any argument for indelible ordination will need to demonstrate how it is consistent with the doctrine of grace, in other words how, appearances notwithstanding, the gift bestowed in ordination may be distinguished from possession.

Several serious issues, like the hearing of the Gospel in a "functional" consumer society, and the understanding of the doctrine of grace, have already begun to emerge as we think about indelibility of orders. Sometimes in the history of the Church a great deal can ride on a seemingly small matter of Church life or practice. What should the date of Easter be? How should monks' tonsure look and what kind of sandals should they wear? Are indulgences allowable as a fund-raising technique? Should we make the sign of the cross? Can we reserve the communion bread? Should worshippers lift their hands in the air? The question of the life-long ordination of priests is such a question for Anglicans today, since it requires articulate answers to a number of other, ultimately more serious, questions. It will prove to be a kind of solvent that brings into clarity other theological commitments previously left murky.

Traditionally, debates about the nature of the priesthood, between Catholic or Protestant, or Anglican and Puritan, were fought, as one would expect, over the proper interpretation of the Scriptures. But at present there is a surprising consensus on the modest amount we can determine about orders from the Scriptures. We can sum up this consensus concisely. First of all, the people of Israel are understood in the revelation at Sinai to be a "priestly people" (see Exod 19:6). From their number a representative few, the sons of Aaron, stood before Yahweh and the people in the priestly role. This pattern of representation continues under the New Dispensation. However, secondly, direct appeal to such passages is not possible for Christians. For the New Testament as a whole, as articulated most clearly in Hebrews, understands Jesus, the great high priest "after the order of Melchizedek," to surpass, fulfill, and so put an end to all other priesthood. He alone stands between God and the people. So no human, including an ordained person, can claim to be a priest straightforwardly, without qualification. What the New Testament does say, thirdly, is that the whole Church (the new Israel) takes on this royal priesthood as it shares by grace in Christ's on-going ministry (1 Pet 2:5), and that a certain few can come to represent the whole Body. So the ordained, from the perspective of the New Testament, can be thought of as priests, but only at a second remove.

When, fourthly, we look at the actual references to ministers in the New Testament, the situation is a fluid one, from which one cannot move directly to any particular Church's structure (as Richard Hooker already understood in the sixteenth century). The clearest and most prominent status is the apostle, the witness to the resurrection of Christ who is sent out as an ambassador for Christ to the nations. Under their authority, and following after them, come "bishops" (*episkopoi*) and "deacons" (*diakonoi*), though there are a number of other ministries, too (see Eph 4:11, for example). The role of the "elder" (*presbuteros*) stands in a murky relation to the others, on occasion appearing to be synonymous with the bishop.[3] At the very least we can say that some ministries seem to depend on special personal gifts (healer, prophet) while others are bestowed, though all depend on the *charismata* of the Holy Spirit. It will be another century and a half before the Church resolves the relationship between the more ordinary and extraordinary gifts (some would say the tension remains in Church history.)[4]

As we consider the early Patristic period, the picture gradually resolves itself. Already at the outset of the second century we see Ignatius of Antioch emphasize the bishop

3. So Acts 20:28 and 1 Pet 5:2–4; see Robert Wright, "The Origins of the Episcopate and Episcopal Ministry in the Early Church," in *On Being A Bishop*, ed. Robert Wright (New York: Church Pension Fund, 1993) 13–14.

4. See Hans von Campenhausen's magisterial *Ecclesiastical Authority and Spiritual Power in the Churches of the First Three Centuries* (Peabody: Hendrickson, 1997).

as focus on unity and spiritual respect in the face of the threat of heresy, with the presbyter and deacon in addition in something already on its way to the threefold ministry.[5] With Irenaeus at the end of the century the place of the bishop, again in connection with the rejection of heresy and the establishment of the creedal faith, is secure.

To be sure, some aspects remain historically unclear. In one place it would seem that the bishop emerged from among the college of elders, and elsewhere the elders seem to have emerged as the bishop's emissaries only slowly. The details of the origins of presbyter and bishop among different ancient Churches may be left to the liturgical historian. But, fifthly, the consistent thing is that, eventually, bishop and presbyter come to be understood in relation to one another (witness the ancient custom of both laying hands on the priest to be ordained), and their special prerogatives include preaching and presiding at the Eucharist.

It is not clear whether in the early period the Church understood orders to be for life. We can at best infer how they would have answered this question. Some presbyters in the Patristic period did leave the work for which they were ordained. But at the same time, the evidence tells us that when they took that work up again, they were not re-ordained. The best we can say, sixthly, is that the practice of

5. Still the offices are types in a way that surprises us: the bishop for God the Father, the presbyters for the apostles, the deacons for Christ.

the early Church was not inconsistent with the belief, later more clearly expressed, that the orders were lifelong.[6]

Out of the historical process came a clear sense of the Church practice for which the priest-bishop is ordained (among other necessary tasks), namely presiding at the Eucharist. This is helpful, for it turns out to be a point of ecumenical agreement. The subsequent history is marked by fierce disagreement between Catholic and Protestant over the nature of the ordained. But both the earlier Catholic tradition and the later Protestant would define the priest in relation to what he (or now she) will do in the liturgy of Word and table. Thomas Aquinas insists that the priest is "ordered" to the end of the celebration of the Eucharist, i.e. the priest is a Eucharist-ward person. Three and a half centuries later the Augsburg Confession will insist that the Church is found wherever the Word is truly preached and the sacraments rightly observed, both tasks belonging to the ordained. They exist in order that the Church might do those acts which make it Church. In other words, both Thomas and Melanchthon (author of the Augsburg Confession) would define the priest/pastor in relation to those basic acts, to Word and table. In this essay we will operate with the assumption that one cannot understand who the ordained is unless we ask what the Church is, for whose order the priest exists. This question in turn can only

6. I have been helped here by a conversation with Dr. John Gibaut of St. Paul University, Ottawa, who is an expert on the development of the concept of orders.

be answered as we look carefully at what happens in true preaching and right celebrating.

This focus on priesthood as an order ordered to the word and sacrament may be shared by Thomas and Melancthon, but it also throws into highlight the most drastic disagreement between the Reformation combatants as well. In fairness, one must bear in mind that Thomas does not set out to place the priest on a pedestal as some kind of superior creature. The thirteenth century village priest, often barely literate, was hardly such. But for Thomas the thing that the priest is to do is so stupendous that even the most learned University of Paris-educated religious would have no better prospects: to turn ordinary bread and wine into the Body and Blood of Christ. This job has no fitting qualifications. How can one do such a thing, even as one quite obviously remains the schlemiel one was before?

Thomas sets about answering this question, to his credit, by going back to the universal Christian inheritance of baptism.[7] He asks himself the (for our purposes pertinent) question: why can't one be baptized a second time? The answer is that the Holy Spirit "seals" us, literally makes an imprint on our souls as one would fix a signet ring into hot wax. That seal is what the Greek (and Latin) term "character" means. In baptism the Holy Spirit acts in so profound a way that we are ever after changed: we may prove to be lousy Christians, but we are Christians nonetheless. To be sure, this baptismal character does not

7. See Thomas Aquinas, *Summa Theologiae* (New York: Benziger, 1948) IIIa Supplement QQ, 34–40.

obliterate our own personalities—we remain ourselves, vices and all. But a dimension of who we are has been added: child of God, inheritor of the Kingdom, recipient of the bread of heaven, etc. So Thomas insisted that all Christians are "ordained" into Christ's royal priesthood in their baptism as a new character is bestowed on them by the Holy Spirit. Because this character is indelible, there can be no rebaptism, even after mortal sin. In other words, to be a baptized Christian is to believe already in the reality of indelible character—one can feel the tight jaws of the Thomistic argument closing in!

In the case of the priest, Thomas simply goes one step further. How can a baptized Christian remain himself, limits and faults and all, and stand at the altar and utter the words *hoc est corpus meum*, "this is my body"? Thomas supposed another gift, following from and additional to that of baptism, a gift also so profound as to mark a character irrevocably "sealed" in the soul. Again it is imagined to be a gift in spite of the person's limitation, one required by the stupendous nature of the sacramental gift. Here the character bestowed is the specific capacity to receive the power required for priestly acts, and in particular transubstantiation of the Eucharistic elements.

Even when the Thomistic argument, laying out the classic Catholic case, is placed in its best light, one can discern some obvious problems. It presumes a view of the Eucharist that many would not share. It casts the argument for priestly character in terms of the reception of a unique power, and, however much one strives to mitigate and qualify, such couching in terms of power has its dangers. In the popular mind a priest so understood runs the risk of being seen as, literally, a potentate. We need different footing on which to set our argument for character than that of a special power residing in the priest.

This sort of squeamishness toward the Thomistic argument is typical of Protestant worries about indelible character. But we cannot so easily reject the initial bases on which Thomas built: the baptismal precedent and the supreme Eucharistic moment. In the first we see what the priest shares with all his or her fellow Christians, and in the latter we see what sets the priest apart. But what is that latter something? How can we defend indelibility, perhaps appealing to character in a different way, and yet avoid the pitfalls of Thomas' classic argument?

Here we may find an important precedent for Anglican theology in the classic study of ecclesiology, the doctrine of the Church, *The Gospel and the Catholic Church*,[8] by Archbishop Michael Ramsey. There he deliberately sets out to offer an understanding of the Church which is ecumenically available, one that makes sense to both Catholic and evangelical.[9] To accomplish this he seeks to give an

8. Michael Ramsey, *The Gospel and the Catholic Church* (London: SPCK, 1990).

9. Moberley's *Ministerial Priesthood* (London: SPCK, 1969) led the way in seeking to move beyond the impasse of Catholic and Protestant perceptions. His proposal begins a family of solutions, to which this essay is related. However I would find the notion of a representative priest acting for (though not on behalf of) the laity still to be a risk to the *solus sacerdos* nature of Christ, and the ecclesiology behind it too much conceived as an *incarnatio elongata*. For a

evangelical argument for a catholic structure, namely the corporate and ordered understanding of the Church. He asks the evangelical question first: what is the Gospel? Then he seeks to show how the relentless pursuit of that question leads to the affirmation of the "Catholic" understanding of the Church. In Ramsey-esque spirit, defenders of the Anglican-Lutheran concordat start with the evangelical content of the apostolic inheritance and work their way to a defense of episcopal succession.[10]

Could one do something similar in the case of indelible priesthood?[11] Could one give arguments which

---

thorough and helpful treatment of Moberly's contribution see David Cox, *Priesthood in a New Millennium: Toward an Understanding of Anglican Presbyterate in the Twenty-First Century* (New York: Church Publishing, 2004). What Ramsey added was the intention to think one's way to the catholic conclusion along an evangelical path. By so doing he grasped the need to offer an apology for the *concreta* of the tradition, lest the evangelical arguments be misconstrued in a way prejudicial to definite ecclesial content.

10. See Ephraim Radner and Russell R. Reno, eds., *Inhabiting Unity: Theological Perspectives on the Proposed Lutheran-Episcopal Concordat* (Grand Rapids: Eerdmans, 1995).

11. Grayson Carter in his *Anglican Evangelicals: Protestant Secessions from the Via Media, c. 1800–1850* (Oxford: Oxford University Press, 2001) helpfully rehearses the history of the question of indelibility in Anglicanism: its affirmation by Hooker, its inclusion in canon law in 1604, and its support even by some evangelicals, no less than John Wesley being among them (381–82). But in the midst of the party conflict of the nineteenth century it came to be a weapon against evangelicals who wished to leave the established Church, and so they turned against the doctrine. Some interestingly argued that ordination was only indelible for those truly called by God! For our purposes the polemical nature of the issue in that era only confirms our project of giving an evangelical argument for a catholic practice.

appeal to the heart of the Gospel itself to defend orders, traditionally understood, without claiming that such orders are themselves mandated by Scripture? Can one chart an evangelical course leading to the predetermined catholic harbor? And if one can't do this for indelible orders, why should we have them?

After reviewing the barrage of theological argument and counter-argument throughout history, someone might well object that ordination for life is just what we Anglicans do, and that is the end of the matter. This seemingly mugwumpish answer is wiser than it first appears, for practice does proceed, with reasons running along after. Furthermore, the practice endures long after the reasons are forgotten. It is felicitous that our practices do not have to give an account of themselves annually, since our resources of theological imagination are often depleted. Still, we live in a time of constant liturgical revision, and sooner or later what we cannot justify may not survive. Practice proceeds, but reasons had better, sooner or later, come running after.

Why priests for life? This essay will endeavor to answer the question in three ways, each answer reinforcing its fellows. Whether this will be the threefold cord that cannot be broken, or a case akin to rabbinic arguments which give a plentitude of answers out of worry that no one will suffice, the reader must determine! At any rate, each argument will first back up and answer the prior question: what is the Church? To be a priest is to be in orders to what? For this essay assumes that asking and answering the question about the priesthood as a free-standing question, without backing up for this prior, more basic question about the nature of the Church, is to invite misunderstanding. Starting with the nature of the Church will, however, require that we wander afield into wider issues. Each chapter will then seek to provide an evangelically catholic answer to the basic ecclesiological question, in the spirit of Ramsey. Each chapter will assume all the preliminaries this introduction has set forth. We will then seek to show it is fitting that orders in a Church of the sort we argue for should be for life. It is hoped that in addressing this one, focused question about orders we will prove to have answered more along the way.

An ecumenical word at the outset is in order. This essay, conceding all the concerns and making all the assumptions delineated in this introductory chapter, defends lifelong orders. In so doing, it does not argue that this is the only possibility, nor that Churches lacking indelibility are not Churches after all. The practice as found in the Anglican tradition does precede its rationale, and I hope the reasons that follow do make a strong supporting case. Other traditions may achieve these same ends in other ways, or this argument may challenge them—that is for them to decide. Here a tradition holding to the threefold indelible ministry seeks only to justify itself.

We began this introduction by mentioning a number of contemporary conundra surrounding ordination, one of which is the debate between "ontological" and "functional" views of the role, as well the manner in which our culture lists toward the functional. One might wonder on which side of this divide the answer of this essay will fall. On this point we do well at the outset to pause for a moment. I take a job as a teacher, so "teacher" describes who I am, but in a way which, in terms of this debate, falls on the "functional" side. On the other hand I am mortal, and we understand this adjective to reside squarely on the "ontological" side, for it is irreversibly and constitutively a part of who I am as a human being. But if we compare the two for a moment, we see that the difference consists precisely in the permanence of the state, which is to say its *indelibility*. It turns out that the question before us, lifelong orders, restates the being-function question in a manner which gets to the heart of the matter. So, by this account, even if a particular view should conceive of the priesthood in terms of its role for a community, in giving a cogent case for its indelibility it shows itself to be an "ontological" argument for orders.

There is a great deal of talk these days about "practices," the younger sibling of the talk about "praxis" a decade or more ago. A practice is a complex activity whose accomplishment proves "its own reward." It requires a series of virtues for its accomplishment, as well as a community within whose story it has meaning.[12] Practices are, in other words, actions which are bundled together with their own intellectual justifications and accompanying moral qualities. Practices remind us that ideas do not float free, but

12. Here I am relying on the definitive account of practices by Alasdair MacIntyre; see his *After Virtue: A Study in Moral Theory* (Notre Dame: University of Notre Dame Press, 1984). "Praxis" carries more Marxist baggage than the more popular contemporary term.

spring forth in particular communities. The holy grail of theological education and reflection is integration of "head and heart," of individual and community, and the idea of a practice captures just such integration. It is worth noting, in passing, that this essay approaches a range of more general questions about the Church by means of reflection on a single, quite specific practice, especially in one branch of the Church. Long before such a word became popular, theologians, and in particular Anglicans, have set about their task in this manner. Perhaps this essay serves as a case in point of such an approach, and the reader may assess its merits and demerits.

Finally, we need to say a word about our title. Our Lord tells us in the Sermon on the Mount that the Church must be salt, and must beware lest it lose that salt and so deserve trampling. Holy orders ought to be salt for the Church, and ought to have this same fear of losing their saltiness.[13] But does this saltiness adhere to priestly identity, to who priests are? How can they *be* salt? That question, raising the possibilities of judgment and renewal, lies at the heart of our inquiry.

13. Salt is also an element in the Aaronic priesthood in Num 18:19 ("this is a perpetual covenant of salt," his translation), an insight gained from T. F. Torrance. It is worth noting that the covenant of salt was for the sake of those whose task it was to protect and guard the atoning sacrifice. As we shall argue in the first chapter, such is the role of the ordained, so long as we understand that sacrifice to be Christ's, once and for all.

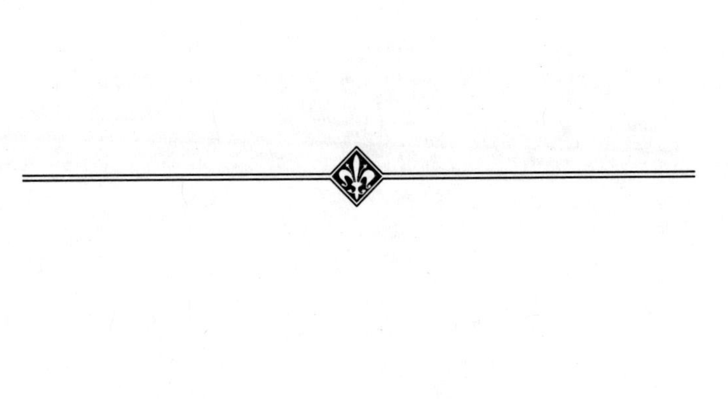

1
The Priest as Counter-Symbol

ROBED SUBVERSIVES

As a missionary priest in the American Southwest, I once attended a rain dance on a Hopi mesa. In the village square, under a sweltering sun, a hundred massive, grave men in kachina masks, skins, evergreens, and bells danced and intoned solemn chants. At the same time, about the edges of the sacred phalanx, were *koshare*, equally sacred clowns, with bodies painted in black and white stripes, with silly hats on their heads and chunks of watermelon in their hands. They irreverently mimicked their priestly colleagues and made obscene gestures to any visitor who seemed prone to embarrassment. For the Hopi the sacred event comprised the whole scene, the dancers and their attendant comics. My point is not to offer some grand generalization about religion, but only to note how, sometimes, religious rituals include built-in means of their own deflation. Different traditions surely have their own reasons and methods at once to affirm and to undercut the point of their ritual. In each case it is a most interesting question to ask why they do this: is it to inculcate humility? Is it part of the message itself?

Rituals at once inflating and deflating may be found in the Christian tradition as well. In the medieval monastery, on the Feast of Fools, in the midst of the sanctity of Lent, for one day, everything became topsy-turvy: the Mass was done backwards, the abbot cleaned the stalls and the novice governed, etc. Or think of Ash Wednesday, when our faces are smudged with soot so that we can stand and hear Jesus, in the Gospel of Matthew, tell us not to disfigure our faces. Both these, admittedly minor, examples, show how, in the liturgy and community, a message can be at once conveyed and eviscerated.

Here we can profitably introduce a concept from contemporary anthropology which has been of service to the study of liturgics.[1] Central to the thought of Victor Turner has been the contrast between structure, the normal order in societies and their rituals, and anti-structure, the moments in which this structure is dissolved, with its resulting features of anarchy, festivity, and communal equality. Such periods of anti-structure may serve to lessen pressures, ease change, or highlight the real purpose for which the structure itself exists. In the midst of the calendar of ordinary time comes Mardi Gras, with its celebration and license, a moment of anti-structure (in this case embedded amidst the structure of time itself). Turner describes the periods

1. See, e.g., Marion J. Hatchett, *Sanctifying Life, Time, and Space: An Introduction to Liturgical Study* (New York: Seabury, 1976).

and persons embodying anti-structure as "liminal" (from the Latin for a doorway), for they reside neither here nor there, but in-between.[2] The example of Feast of Fools is just such a moment of liminality, in which anti-structure has broken into the rigid structure of monastic life, not to destroy the latter, but rather to renew it by reminding all in humility of the end toward which the structure exists (i.e., humble service).

THE CRANMERIAN NON-SACRIFICE

With occasions of ritual evisceration of meaning, and the interpretive category of anti-structure in mind, consider the following example found closer to home. According to the rite prescribed in the *Book of Common Prayer*, the celebrant-priest stands before the congregation during the Great Thanksgiving of the Eucharist. He or she proceeds, in the insistent language of Thomas Cranmer,

2. The most classic work is Victor Turner, *The Ritual Process: Structure and Anti-structure*, The Lewis Henry Morgan Lectures (New York: Aldine de Gruyter, 1995). In citing Turner I follow along the path which Urban Holmes's works mapped out, though with a purpose and a destination diametrically opposed to that of the experientialist Holmes. On this see Leander Harding, "What Have We Been Telling Ourselves About Priesthood?," *Sewanee Theological Review* 43, no. 2 (2000) 144–66. As Clifton Guthrie points out in "Sacral Power: A De-centered Theology of Clergy Authority" (PhD dissertation, Emory University, 1996) Holmes was indeed interested in a "de-centering" of clerical authority, and this would seem to bear a resemblance to our argument, but the telling question is of course "re-centered on what?," and Holmes's answer was radically different from ours.

to deny that any offering or sacrifice is being made, that in fact the one, true, only "sacrifice, oblation, and satisfaction" has already been accomplished on the cross of Christ. Having made this abundantly and repeatedly clear, the priest confirms that the people are making a sacrifice, one of responding praise and thanksgiving. Likewise as the consecration prayer continues, we are told again that ". . . we are unworthy to offer any sacrifice," and yet at the end of the prayer we are reminded in Paul's words from Rom 12:1 that our lives must be a "reasonable, holy, and living sacrifice." The prayer, in other words, plays a kind of spiritual shell-game, giving and taking away the language of sacrifice and offering. The person at the table looks and acts priestly, and does seemingly priestly things (e.g., spreading hands over the gifts) even as he or she reiterates its denial. Something complex is afoot here, for the meaning is conveyed precisely by the stronger, intellectually prior denial of sacrifice in tandem with the form of offering itself. The liturgy acts out its non-sacrifice by way of pointing to the real sacrifice, and so of indicating that a secondary, personal kind of sacrifice is called for as well.

What are we to make of the Cranmerian priest in the middle of all this to and fro? One must bear in mind the great story which is being conveyed to the worshipper by means of the whole Eucharistic event, the story of the saving death and resurrection of Jesus. He is the true prophet, priest, and king by means of those events, narrated for us in the Gospels. But He fulfills these offices in the most surprising and counter-intuitive ways. He is proven king as he surrenders all power in obedience to His heavenly Father. He is the true priest even as He himself is killed, at which moment the Temple is rent (and so, symbolically, the whole sacrificial system comes to an end). He is the true prophet even as His own disciples sleep and eventually flee (so that He is not yet truly heard). He Himself is king, priest, prophet in disturbing ways that undo the pre-existing orders of rule and sacrifice in the very moment that true rule and sacrifice are established.

The priest who stands at the table and reads that communion prayer, in the service of this surprising Priest and King, in spite of all appearing, reinforces that he or she is neither, all in the service of pointing to Him. And by so doing he or she is proven a fitting symbol of priestly offering (of one's self, one's life, etc.) He or she is, then, a kind of counter-symbol that preserves the form of the signified (i.e. priesthood), even as it works to undercut his or her own claim. And all this is done to the service of the One who is the real and only Priest, who redefines, fulfills, and ends all priesthood in Himself. The minister at the table is a counter-sign that works by its own displacement, by becoming a great finger stretched away from oneself and toward the dying Jesus at the center of the Church's life (as the great triptych by Gruenewald depicts).

Does such a Cranmerian priest represent structure or anti-structure, in Victor Turner's terms? As a regular religious servant taking part in a standardized ritual he or she is clearly embedded in the structure, but in such a way that, by the ritual's very design and intent, he or she serves by displacing, reordering, undercutting, in sum by being a built-in element of anti-structure. So the priest in the Cranmerian rite is, in form, a symbol, and in content, a counter-symbol, both taken together accomplishing a task of pointing away toward the one who is the one Great High Priest.

Such an understanding of the priest, as the one who points away from oneself to the true Priest, will only take us so far. For it remains at a level of formality, as if all one had to do to be a valid priest would be to point away from oneself. A pervasive problem for the theology of priesthood is in fact the undue dependence on formal definitions. The valid priest is . . . the one ordained with the proper Episcopal hands, or the one blessed with the proper invocation of the Holy Spirit, or, in more recent times, the one with the properly pastoral, or professional, or imaginative credentials, or whatever. There are many such definitions of the priest, and each has something to commend it, and yet each leaves the diner strangely famished an hour later. Our initial try at a definition differs in specifics, but not in kind, from such definitions. What is lacking in such proposals?

Here we may appeal to the analogous debate over "apostolic succession" between Anglicans and Lutherans in their dialogue in recent years. Anglicans have preferred to define the apostolic in relation to traditional formal structures of the Church, while Lutherans have sought to turn the conversation back to the apostles' teaching, to the content of the Gospel in whose faithful transmission the apostolic is to be found. Something similar may be noted here. Can we really talk of valid priesthood in terms of the form of ministry apart from what actual content, what actual teaching and proclaiming, is being pointed *to*? The priesthood is by its very nature an ironic office, a role of self-evacuation by which the priest points away—but toward what? That makes all the difference.

The short, and obvious, answer is Jesus Christ risen and present both in the Word the priest truly proclaims and the sacrament he or she rightly observes, for it is, after all, *His* Word and *His* table. Well, of course. But this answer has more bite than we would at first acknowledge or perceive. We can look at the matter from two perspectives or two levels. Let us begin with the popular level, that of the ordinary parish.

WITNESSES BY GRACE TO THE RISEN ONE

Priest and parish are caught up with the fall festival, the deficit, and the personal crises of several members. These issues of community life consume those most committed to its welfare. For reasons good and not so good, attention is drawn by a kind of inertia toward the members themselves and their concerns. It takes a deliberate effort, a being roused from sleep, to recall Whose the parish is. The problem is compounded by commendable impulses of the contemporary Church. We affirm that all have gifts and encourage each to discern them at workshops. Some celebrate progress in social justice, others charisms of the Spirit, others lay ministry itself, others Enneagram and Myers-Briggs, yet others spiritual experience or psychological insight. All these may be goods, but to put them first, or to focus attention on them overmuch tends to a preoccupation, not with God the giver, but ourselves. Their celebration amounts, in theological terms, to what Martin Luther called a "theology of glory,"[3] which does not start with God as He chooses to be known in Jesus' cross. As a result, this overemphasis on charisms conduces to a theology of our own efforts at cross-purposes to a theology of grace.

In contrast the priest must be the one who often moves the congregation against the grain, by witnessing on their behalf against their own preoccupations. He or she must stand often at the parish's margin in the sense that he or she points away from them and toward their source and prime agent, Jesus Christ. This pointing may work itself out in prosaic ways such as claiming time in the vestry meeting full of roofs and conflicts for prayerful attention to Christ's Lordship over the parish.

A similar kind of distinction may be found at the more abstract and seemingly rarified level of theology. Let us assume for argument's sake that there is a profound disagreement in contemporary theology between "revisionist" and "traditional" approaches. There have been prolonged disagreements about where to place the real fault-line between these kinds of theology. Some say that the telling difference is that some emphasize human experience

3. See Martin Luther, "The Heidelberg Disputation," in *Martin Luther's Basic Theological Writings*, ed. Timothy F. Lull (Minneapolis: Fortress, 1989) 30–49.

as opposed to Scripture. Or the key difference might be that some theologies are anthropocentric (centered on human realities) while others are theocentric (centered in the prior reality of God). Others find the key difference in the preference for symbol over narrative. Others think the dividing line is between those who resist authority per se, and those who assume it. Still others find the fatal flaw in the pursuit of some neutral, prior, objective norm for truth by which Biblical claims can be measured, which others in turn reject. Ways to slice the theological cake could be multiplied.

The chasm between types of theology is best mapped along another fault-line—the "real presence" of the person Jesus Christ as the One to whom the Church's prayers are addressed. All Christian talking and praying address Jesus Christ, but what purpose does He then serve for their theologies? On the one hand are theologians for whom "Christ is risen" serves primarily as a symbol, exemplification, illustration, or (to use Rahner's favorite term) a thematization of something else, human authenticity, or hope, or struggle against oppression, or whatever. The priest ends up pointing, not to Christ, but through Him, toward that to which Christ Himself points. The theologian understands the Christian prayers on which he or she reflects as expressions of hope or exhortation to these various forms of "something else." "Jesus Christ is risen today" amounts to "good triumphs over evil," or "pursue the truth, no matter what," or "the future belongs to divine justice," etc. Descriptions of Jesus are really descriptions of ourselves.

By contrast the theologian can take as basic to his or her reflection the fact that Christians address their prayers *to a Person*, Jesus Christ.[4] This in turn means that Jesus is alive, that He is an agent in His own right, and that language addressed to Him, must, for all its subtleties, be understood in a realist manner. It means that who and what Jesus is cannot be so readily absorbed into who and what we are. Where Christian talk is understood truly as address, then there is someone else with whom we have to deal, the shepherd of our souls. This does not mean, of course, that it is easy or clear what such new, resurrected life is for Jesus, or what it shall mean for us. That Jesus risen is present is the starting point for reflection, but how He is present will be a matter for debate until He returns in a manner clear to all.

This line of demarcation is nothing new, although it has been expressed in different terms in different ages. Throughout Christian history the Church has struggled over various issues which it has perceived to be of life-or-death importance. In each case the real, underlying issue has been the serious assumption of the risen, reigning Jesus in the Church. The New Testament itself bears evidence of the struggle over grace and works in the Gentile Churches of Paul's provenance—if Jesus is really raised and reigning, then God has acted decisively for the salvation of all, the new aeon has come, and the time to flow

4. I am indebted on this point, as are a number of my generation who studied at Yale Divinity School, to the insight of Robert Johnson about the crucial divide in modern theology.

to Zion is now. In the early Church, the struggle with the Arians was a struggle about Christ's full divinity—if Jesus is raised and personally present, then He is one with the Creator who alone gives and redeems life. In the Middle Ages, Christians debated whether Christ was present in the Eucharist symbolically or physically—if Jesus is truly present in the midst of the worshippers, then He is free to be in the elements fully, and to work through them as well. In the time of the Reformation, the debate is about the sufficiency of grace alone through faith—if Jesus is raised and present, then He has the power to initiate and to complete the work of salvation for us. The assumption of the realistic presence of Another, Christ, in our midst, may be seen as the heart of the matter behind a series of varied disputes in Christian history.

Priests are not systematic theologians, nor do they serve primarily as theological censors. But they do exist, within the Church, as an order charged to remind of and defend something definite, something so central as to be indispensable—the real presence of the risen and reigning Christ Jesus in the midst of the community. To reiterate, their role in the Church cannot be adequately accounted for in merely formal terms, but must include this material claim and all that follows from it. This real and personal presence is the "one thing needful," so that the Church remains the Church.

As we have shown, both the common experience of the parish and the debate of the academy conspire toward the same end, that this real presence of Christ risen should be central. For in both theological reflection and parish practice, this claim is endangered anew by multifarious ways in which we humans would make our own effort or experience the spiritual starting-point. In both thought and action, we are always in danger of justifying ourselves, to guard against which priests exist as the order dedicated to justification by faith in Christ, who is really risen and present. Again, the priest cannot be understood or defined in some neutral or formal way, but only as he or she points away from themselves and toward Someone definite, Jesus risen.

We can now see an additional sense in which priesthood is an *order*. For by this ministry the Church intends to keep not only its own life, but also the truth it proclaims, in right order. The reality of Christ risen and present comes first. It is, in the expression of St. Thomas Aquinas, the *prima veritas*, the truth that must precede. In its light the Church proceeds to see and understand everything else in its life. Priesthood exists to keep first things first, to allow the One who precedes (or, in the language of the Book of Common Prayer, "prevents") all its own effort that pride of place. It is an order of persons in service of a proper order of truth and of reflection on that truth.

By such a definition we can see the ordained as the rightful followers of the unique ministry of the apostles. For they were first of all witnesses to the resurrection of Jesus.[5]

5. This insight is found in Wolfhart Pannenberg, *The Church*, trans. Keith Crim (Philadelphia: Westminster, 1983). See the chapter titled "The Significance of Eschatology for an Understanding of the

Paul reminds of this in 1 Cor 15:3–11, where he cites the apostles as among those who first saw the risen Christ, and mentions his own status as an apostle in connection with his vision of the Risen One, even if as "one lately born . . ." (my translation). Or one may consider the opening verses of 1 John, where the apostle is the one who tells of what has been seen, heard, touched, the bodily risen One. Or we may think of the great commission at the conclusion of Matt 28:16–20, where the risen Christ sends the apostles out to teach and baptize on the basis of their encounter with Him. To the apostolate there is a very definite content and a very personal reference; bishops first, and in their stead priests as well, exist to ensure that the Church as a whole continues this witness.

By this logic, one who denies the truth of Christ's resurrection, or His living presence with the community, is simply no priest at all. The atheist priest in the footsteps of Don Cupitt, and the pluralist priest following the teaching of a John Hick (for whom Christ is emblematic of a more generic divine saving power) are walking oxymorons. There can be no dichotomy between the order of truth and holy orders, the latter existing to subserve the former. The apostolic succession of ministry exists for the sake of the apostolic inheritance of the truth.

A good passage of Scripture to consider in this regard is Eph 4:1–12, where the triumphant, ascended Christ sends down on the Church gifts for the variety of ministries. The latter are only possible because of that victory,

---

Apostolicity and Catholicity of the Church."

and are themselves the prizes coming from "taking captivity captive." These ministries in turn are to build up the one Body of Christ by means of sound doctrine, so that mature spiritual growth is possible for the community as a whole. Here ministry is securely ordered so as to follow from the person of the ascended Christ and to subserve the upbuilding in love of the whole.

Let us summarize the conclusions we have reached so far. The priest is the member of the Church charged with the task of pointing away from himself or herself so as to point toward the One by whom and for whom the Church exists, the risen and present Jesus Christ. He or she serves as a referent to Him. He or she does this by presenting the form of the priest, at the same time he or she undercuts the substantive priestly claim. So we might say that the leader in the Christian community has to know what priesthood is, to know how indispensable it is, and finally to know most definitively that he or she does not possess it. Thus she or he does not have a priestly ministry, so much as a priestward one, a ministry of redirection, recasting, and escort.[6]

What sort of definition of priesthood have we offered? It is not a definition couched in terms of power or a specific

6. John Webster's argument for an ostensive or indicative understanding of ordained ministry moves in a similar direction to this essay. As always he is keen to protect the sovereignty of Christ to establish the community oriented to Him, but not thereby to be trapped by it. In other words, he too would seek a truly evangelical theology of orders. See "The Self-Organizing Power of the Gospel of Christ: Episcopacy and Community Formation," in *Word and Church: Essays in Church Dogmatics* (Edinburgh: T. &T. Clark, 2001) 208ff.

faculty, as in the traditional Thomist view. It is more akin to definitions of the priest as icon, such as one would find in the Orthodox tradition. (This iconic understanding is the reason, for example, that priests cannot have visible physical deformities in that tradition,[7] though obviously the present treatment holds no sympathy for that feature.) The priest is a symbol, first of all of the faithful themselves. The priest exists to show the Church something *about itself*, to reflect back its proper and necessary nature as a body turned toward Jesus Christ. The priest is not an icon of Christ, but rather of the Church as it seeks to attend to, imitate, be, the Body of Christ.[8] So we might then say that the priest is a kind of metonymy for the Church, a part meant on a variety of occasions to stand in for the whole, and it is a kind of mnemonic, a reminder of true identity.[9] This notion of being a sign for the faithful themselves will be an idea that we shall pick up and develop further in the next chapter and its second approach to the question of priesthood.[10]

7. See Thomas Hopko's article in *To Be A Priest: Perspectives on Vocation and Ordination*, eds. Robert E. Terwilliger and Urban T. Holmes (New York: Seabury, 1975).

8. A similar point may be found in L. William Countryman's study of the theology of ordination, *The Language of Ordination: Ministry in an Ecumenical Context* (Philadelphia: Trinity, 1992), although he does not add the aspect of pointing away from oneself toward Christ.

9. In answer to the technical question, the priest by this account is *in persona ecclesiae* rather than *in persona Christi*, though the element of nuance comes in the fact that the *ecclesia* is defined by its attention to its Lord.

10. My appeal to the concept of a sign was informed by Bishop

But how is this to be accomplished? By saying that the priest is to be a symbol, we do not have in mind only his or her sacramental role, as the president for the assembly in public worship. We do not mean that he or she is an icon only in the literal and visual sense, though this is indeed one part of his or her role. Rather, the place to start in thinking about the priest as an "indicative" symbol is with the great treasure-trove of symbols, the Scriptures. The priest is sign most properly as he or she utters, explains, and enacts the Word of God. She or he is most properly a sign in serving the true signs of His presence, the canonical words of the Old and New Testaments. For in this activity the priest stands in the sacred grove of signs, and delights to graze there.[11] There the role of all the signs, first written, also living, to point out and raise up Christ, is clearest. We need to develop our theology of priest as symbol in the closest relationship to our theology of the Word, and so to see how he or she is a Word-symbol, a sacred semaphore.[12]

SYMBOLS OF THE WORD LIVING AND ACTIVE

An adequate theology of the Word, especially in relation to the priest as its servant, emphasizes its comprehensiveness. The Word in its fullness has to be expressed in the Church: as word preached and sacrament celebrated, as semantic

---

Stephen Sykes's "The Apostolicity of Bishop and People as a Sign of the Kingdom of God," in *Inhabiting Unity*. See Introduction, note 10, for complete citation.

11. The image is found in Augustine's *Confessions,* XI.3.

12. The phrase is Rowan Williams's.

meaning and the event of its utterance. It is in this fuller sense that we can see the ministry of the priest as integral to the proclamation of the Word. Making the Word central does not mean elevating the pulpit over the table. The Word is better understood if the sermon is its sacrament in airwaves, and the latter is the Word affixed to the elements so as to make His presence bodily immediate. The priest's ministry as both preacher and celebrant can then be understood under the category of the Word. As our citations of Cranmer's Eucharistic prayer should remind us, both pulpit and table serve to point away from themselves to Him, and precisely in so doing prove sacramental.

An eloquently evangelical understanding of the priesthood in relation to the Word may be found in Thomas Torrance's *Royal Priesthood: A Theology of Ordained Ministry,*[13] where he includes this same comprehensive view of word and sacrament. Torrance begins by showing how the Israelite priesthood was at its core a ministry of the Word. He proceeds to show how the incarnation of the Word fulfills these priestly hopes, at once embodying the divine blessing and human faithfulness. The risen Christ is the one who has created a new time and space for the Church, between ascension and Parousia, and thereby has given us access to the Father. Through the Word He communicates to us and gives us this access in fulfillment of His priestly ministry. This Word-centered understanding is not over again a sacramental one, but rather places the latter in its proper perspective. Torrance puts the matter this way:

13. *Royal Priesthood* (Edinburgh: T. & T. Clark, 1983).

"the sacraments span the two moments of the first Advent and the moment of the final Advent. The sacraments do not add anything to the Word of forgiveness but they are that Word in complete and full event." The priest is given a share in this full ministry of the Word.

This comprehensive view also comprises Word as meaning and as event. We can go on to say that in the case of the ordained, the very identity of the minister, the person they are in the community, communicates and bodies forth the Word for their fellows. Here we do well to recall that Luther himself (in certain moods at least) included a third dominical sacrament alongside font and table, namely the power of the keys, the privilege of pronouncing the words of absolution. This act too is reserved to the ordained. For Luther the high importance of the keys followed from the centrality of the justification of the ungodly, the doctrine on which the Church stands or falls. This power does not reside in any sense in the ordained, and yet the word of forgiveness must be uttered, it must be heard from without by the sinner, and the task of this utterance is reserved to the priest. He or she exists in the Body as the one who utters Christ's forgiveness. This task epitomizes the symbol that is the whole life of the priest.

At this point the kind reader still waits patiently for the promised answer. For we have not yet shown why a priest, understood in this iconic way, could not serve for a season and then give way to a fellow priest equally committed to this symbolic ministry on behalf of the whole. Why must one be an icon for life? Here we must recall that the priest is charged with reminding the community of the One who is graciously present, that is, whose presence depends not on their efforts, prayers, or conjuring. In this regard we bear in mind the tendencies the priest needs to point away from. Throughout the Church's life, the gravitational pull of works-righteousness is felt. In the parish the prime tendencies come down to function and management, in the religious academy to experience: they are all species of works in the modes of doing and having.

Priesthood can only symbolize this state of receiving who we are as a gift if the identity is not lodged in our wills, our career plans, or own efforts. The priest can only evacuate attention from his or her own accomplishments and efforts if the symbolic role itself is, by contrast, permanent. Pointing away from itself and toward Christ is who the Church is, and so its metonymy too, the priest, must be so as well. From this perspective too we can see that the special gift of the Holy Spirit for ordained ministry is an ironic one, for it guards against the greater temptation to suppose that we clergy stand by virtue of something possession superadded to us.

We began by asserting that we can only understand priesthood as we ask what the Church is. Conversely we can see more of the true nature of the Church as we see rightly the priesthood. The very discipline of ecclesiology, of theological reflection on the nature of the Church, is a post-Reformation phenomenon. One searches the *Summa Theologiae* for the articles on the nature of the Church. Grace, sacraments, orders, are there, yes, but the surrounding medium of the Church in which they all exist is as invisible to Thomas as water is to a fish. So it should be, for some realities can only be seen clearly and accurately in our peripheral vision. When we look straight at them, the act of looking distorts their appearance. The Church is such a thing, truly seen as we look away and focus solely on who Jesus Christ is. Then the Church appears at the edges of our vision as the manger, the mount, the boat, in which he lies. It is properly a shy subject, fittingly so since it is the Temple of the shy member of the Trinity, the Holy Spirit. The priest, in his or her own person, quite apart from his or her efforts (though not apart from their proclaiming), is the fitting sign for such a peripheral reality.

"AS ONE WITH AUTHORITY . . ."

The interpretation of priesthood offered in this, our first argument is iconic, kenotic, verging on the parodic. But does this mean that priesthood so understood does not bear real authority? Or is the priest spending so much time deferring and begging-your-pardon-sir for the proper role that he or she cannot fulfill it? To answer this question we need a clear notion of the authority we imagine they should have. We may think of authority, in distinction from sheer power, as a rightful claim, growing from inherent qualities or stature, which someone has on the response of another. So long as he is not a despot, the king as king has a claim, and likewise the sage, by virtue of the truthfulness of his judgment, also has a claim. The nature of each claim is appropriate to the kind of inner resource he or she has, in one case a rank to which the subject has sworn allegiance, in the other, a correspondence of thought with how things really are that demands acknowledgment. So what kind of authority does the priest have? What is the inner possession calling for the legitimate response?

Here several of the major ecumenical documents of our time, addressing the underlying question of authority, can help us. *Baptism, Eucharist, and Ministry* offers an account of the pastoral office friendly to the argument of this essay: the ordained are "publicly and continually responsible for pointing to (the church's) fundamental dependence on Jesus Christ."[14] In other words, a distinctively Christian account of authority will follow the same pattern of divine initiative and human response which guides this argument as well. Authority must first be defined with respect to Jesus Christ alone, for He as Word is the divine *auctor* and He has done the decisively saving deed to which the Church is obliged to offer its "Amen."[15] So argues the Anglican-Roman Catholic *The Gift of Authority*. The Church exercises legitimate authority as it points toward its Lord as the Body's Head, and in so doing claims a derivative and dependent authority. The definition of the ordained is the definition of authority, couched in terms of a person.

Here we should distinguish between what in sum the priest does, namely point away from oneself to Christ, and

14. World Council of Churches, *Baptism, Eucharist, and Ministry*, 11. I am indebted in this section to Robert Jenson's *Unbaptized God* (Minneapolis: Augsburg, 1992) 51 and 57.

15. Anglican/Roman Catholic International Commission, *The Gift of Authority* (Toronto: ABC, 1999).

the means by which he or she does this in the actual life of a parish. The latter will assume forms that involve no little self-assertion. The major form is catechesis, at once adaptable, patient, listening, and yet also willing to be definite as to conclusions when doctrine is at stake. On occasion the pastor may need to exhort,[16] when there is conflict in the parish, or to admonish, when a parishioner is engaged in behavior destructive of himself or another. Perhaps the jargon of "tough love" will make the task more acceptable. But in each case the pastor bears in mind how different these activities are from the willfulness of authoritarianism. To indulge one's own private judgments, or to suppose that all opinions are equal in an endless dialogue, or to shrink back from parish conflict in avoidance, or to offer a blander kind of acceptance when confrontation is called for: these are all forms of failing to point to the authoritative One, and so of ceding authority to the community on its own terms or its surrounding culture. The harder road, the doctrinally and ethically assertive one, far from being the abrogation of power to the priest himself or herself, is actually the costly pointing away toward the One who truly holds the plumbline for the community.

16. See Rowan Williams on reclaiming the Exhortation of the Book of Common Prayer Communion service in "Imagining the Kingdom: some questions for Anglican worship today," in *The Identity of Anglican Worship*, eds. K. Stevenson and B. Spinks (Harrisburg, PA: Morehouse, 1991).

2
The Priest as the Sign of the Oath

SUNDAY IN ST. ANYWHERE'S

IT IS THE ORDINARY Sunday morning in the ordinary parish. Ranged around the nave is a crowd of a hundred, some in a small mass in the nearer pews, other scattered with easier access to the door. And who are they that gather this morning? You can predict some sorts and conditions that will be present. Mrs. Memento, in her eighties, has been dying slowly of cancer for a year. Royal, smiling in the front row, has Down Syndrome. Mr. and Mrs. Persevere, old marrieds, can be counted on to come to everything, as does Annie, who lives alone. Zekaria has come recently from Nigeria. And greeting them all is the Rev. Mary Fidelia, the pastor with her harried husband and children in tow. In their idiosyncrasy they are part of the texture of the place, but they are more as well. They are mixed into the motley gang that is the parish, cheek by jowl with several un-baptized who occasionally wander in, as well as others whose personal lives are messier. Then there are those conspicuous to the regulars in their absence, the Irelys who are still fighting with the last rector, the Doles who have fallen away since their son's illness.

What is a parish anyway? It is, by Luther's account, a Mouth-house, a place to speak and hear the Word of God, and to see and receive it ourselves at the Lord's Table. But the Word is represented in a complex manner in a parish. For the family of symbols found in Scripture is not only presented in their speaking, but the hearers themselves body forth Christ the very Word they hear. They must be themselves a field or system of symbols that follow from and are consonant with the symbols they hear in Scripture. They are a series of lights which they shine forth to one another, like a line of lighthouses. This system of symbols reminds one another of the meaning of the Church as it reflects the master symbols of Scripture.[1] Together they show forth the meaning of Christ's Body, first for themselves, and then, collectively, for the world.

What does this mean for our friends, waiting for the liturgy to begin in the nave of St. Anywhere's? They are themselves unique children of God. But once within the assembly of the Body, they take on a series of meanings for one another, their lives serving to represent distinct aspects of the Gospel in the Church. Each meaning is warranted in Scripture, but their lives render those meanings in personal form. To be sure, each must have a moral life of some consistency with their significance as an ecclesial sign, lest they contradict their own given bodily symbol. Some provide a

1. See Austin Farrer, *The Glass of Vision* (London: Dacre, 1948).

more adequate and consonant symbol than others. But still they all have more meaning for one another as Christians, in the Body, than they would simply as an aggregate of individuals.

How would we interpret the Churchmen and Churchwomen we mentioned? Memento means for the Body that this age is passing away, but the new is come (1 Cor 4:16). Royal reminds all that this new covenant community stands before God solely by grace given in God's own call to us, and not by any gift of intelligence or power that we ourselves might possess. (1 Cor 1:26) [2] The Perseveres show forth the mystical love of Christ for His Church, and so have a meaning quite at the heart of the Gospel revelation for the community as a whole (Eph 5:32). Anne on the other hand reminds those who might covet the Perseveres' life, that we of the new Israel now belong finally to God alone (1 Cor 7:32).[3] In a parish otherwise mostly white, Zecharia means for the whole that baptism gathers all the tribes of the Gentiles, in the midst of suffering, to witness and praise the God of Israel in the end-times.

2. David Keck makes a similar point about Alzheimer's as a sign for the Body about our identities as gracious gifts in his *Forgetting Whose We Are: Alzheimer's Disease and the Love of God* (Nashville: Abingdon, 1996).

3. I heard Henri Nouwen make this point in a class I took with him in seminary.

PEOPLE OF THE OATH

Those Christians are gathered as a parish for the celebration of the sacrament of Holy Communion, but what does *that* sort of symbol, a sacrament, mean? In Latin *sacramentum* referred to an oath or pledge. What has drawn those people together, and what keeps them together in spite of the centrifugal force of which fallen creatures are so prone, is the power of the pledge or promise, offered at the Last Supper, sealed in Christ's blood at Golgotha, vindicated on Easter morning. That promise of Christ's is what we call "the new testament," that people of all the earth can be forgiven their sins and restored to God through faith in Christ. The people of St. Anywhere's have gathered in response to that pledge of God's. Properly speaking He alone is fit and able to swear by His own name, and yet in gratitude they have made a responsorial pledge of their own, to follow Christ and to witness to Him even at a cost. They are the baptized, who have taken the solemn oath to renounce their old, alienated, distorted life, and now to live on the basis of the pledge made to them by God.

It is hard for contemporary persons, living in a society given to self-expression and satisfaction, to feel the full weight of pledge making and receiving. The solemnity of the medieval knight's troth, or the exotic power of the blood brotherhood, is the closest we may get to the power an oath should inspire. But that is just the sort of event a baptism is, and all the other sacraments borrow from it the same power of the pledge. "Until we are parted by death . . . this is my solemn vow" say the bride and groom, and we need some insight into the heroic society to understand what terrible words we have uttered. The Christian sacramental life depends for its moral and spiritual seriousness on taking and receiving oaths earnestly.

In fact, one may draw a yet deeper conclusion about the doctrine of the human person from the issue of oaths. The state of a human soul is closely related to its power to collect itself, and apply itself, decisively and once and for all. This power makes freedom of soul possible.[4] We may conclude then that the health of a human soul is its power to make, in seriousness, an oath whereby it defines oneself. We can only have our identity defined as we are summed up in a decisive, and hence, permanent commitment. Likewise our moral health is the sum of the oaths we have taken, broken, kept. In our dotage all else in our life fades from us and is indeed vanity, but in the end, as we survey our lives, they display the moral weight that is the record of our oaths. The rise of divorce in contemporary society is related, among other things, to the loss of a sense of the moral seriousness of oath-taking. To repeat, all Christians know that their oath-making is corrupted by sin, and have taken Christ's oath on their behalf as their own, and conduct their own swearing only in its wake. We have heard and heeded the Second Commandment, and made our oaths in the only manner that is not vain.[5]

4. See Karl Rahner's discussion of this, in existential terms, in *Foundations of Christian Faith: An Introduction to the Idea of Christianity* (New York: Seabury, 1978) 95–96.

5. This has been informed by Dr. Christopher Seitz's talk on oath-making and the Second Commandment at a SEAD (Scholarly

What does this tell us about the symbolic significance bodied forth by the individuals who stand in that Sunday assembly of the baptismally sworn? Each reflects some aspect of the covenantal, baptismal community of Jesus Christ, some feature of the pledged life they all are now called to lead. Not that any stand in for Christ, but the life of each portrays some virtue or aspect of the gracious work of Christ on their behalf as Church. Once they are firmly "in place," then others around the edges of the congregation can come to take on an attenuated or extended meaning as well. The parish forms a grid, a semiotic tree, in which others whose lives are messier and more anomalous can take the shelter of a borrowed meaning, can receive a wider and clearer context for their own broken and partial meaning. The occasional inquirer comes to bespeak the movement of the Spirit quietly drawing the world to Christ. The young couple living together reflect some of the qualities of commitment and affection whose sacramental expression is found in the Perseveres. (To be sure, as individuals it would be better for these to believe rather than temporize, to marry rather than fornicate, but they benefit at the messier penumbra of the community by the sacred context in which they live their lives).

So what finally does the pastor, Mary Fidelia, mean to the whole? The first thing to note is what she does not mean. She is not the sole symbol of the nature of the Church and its life before God. She is one symbol flashing to her broth-

---

Engagement with Anglican Doctrine) Conference in Dallas in March of 2002.

ers and sisters amidst a virtual firestorm of mutual symbols. At the same time her symbolic significance is of an unique kind and importance. She "orders" the others by showing the order that pertains in them all. She is a symbol for and about all the symbols which reflect forth the original signs of Scripture.

While the others point to aspects of the pledged, covenantal community, Mary Fidelia reminds all of the pledge itself as the basis of their community. It is by virtue of this distinction that one can say that she not only points to the sacraments, but also points in her person, after ordination, to *sacramentalitas*, the oathed quality of Christian life itself. She is a sign of God's giving of the pledge itself to the Church (and of its gracious nature, as we saw in the preceding chapter), and also of the avowed life that arises for the Church as a result. As such, her ministry must be lifelong, for that "until we are parted by death . . . this is my solemn vow" quality per se is precisely what she or he bodies forth.

THE *MYSTERION* OF CHRIST AND THE CHURCH

In one of the classic Biblical passages about the pastorate, 1 Tim 3:1–7, we find an emphasis on the need that the orderliness of the bishop's own inner life and his own home reflect the order he would preserve in the community. First of all, the leader must present no *skandalon* to the faithful: he mustn't be greedy or drunken or combative. Thus he must be one who can present the faith to those outside with a "pure conscience" (3:9, KJV). Secondly, the leader must reflect in his own family the orderliness of the household of faith as a whole. Here we go a step deeper into the nature of the calling. The overseer must reflect not one quality of the community among others, but rather the way the whole coheres. His life must be orderly, just as the congregation is orderly (3:5). In this context we find a close connection between exhortation to the ordained and marital status: he must be "the husband of one wife" (3:2, KJV).

This is sound moral advice on its own terms, and it guards the community from scandal. But this last requirement has a deeper symbolic meaning. Here we do well to read the reference to the married status of the bishop in relation to the classic passage on this subject, Eph 5:31–33: "this is a great *mysterion* [mystery? sacrament?], I speak of Christ and the Church" (5:32, my translation). In other words, the sign of the married within the Body, the symbolic valence of the Perseveres, has a role that goes deeply to the heart of the presence of Christ in His Church. For it is a bodily relationship, at the very juncture of creation and new creation (Mark 10:2–9), which is stronger even than death (Song 8:6). While other signs show qualities of Christ's presence, the married couple shows the very depth and duration of the presence of the One who, loving them "to the limit" (John 13:1, my translation), and being raised, is with them "to the end of the age" (Matt 28:20, NRSV).

The bishop/priest likewise exists in the congregation as a symbol of unqualified fidelity, which is to say, of the depth and duration of the covenant love of Christ for His

Church received and responded to in baptism. As such, the symbol of the bishop/priest has a special relationship to the symbol of the married. If we accept this intertwining of symbols, we can see, by means of the intratextual reading offered above, why the seemingly simple requirement, "a man of one wife" takes on deeper resonance. However, at this point an obvious question presents itself: what of the majority of priests in the traditional Churches who observe celibacy in one way or another?[6] Far from contradicting our intertwining, this bolsters it. For the tradition of married priests witnesses to the connection by fulfilling the words of 1 Tim 3:2 directly. But traditions which do not allow priests to marry argue for the marriage of priest to the parish or to the Church. The symbolic connection has an immediate relationship to the prohibition itself. Symbols have a complex logic of their own.

This latter point is bolstered if we look once again at Thomas Aquinas's account of orders, this time with respect to the bishop.[7] His discussion of the subject is found in his treatment of religious states. The placement has to do not only with the fact that bishops were usually monks, but also with the fact that it was itself a religious state, one with its

6. The exception for the Roman Catholics is of course their Uniate branches, and for the Orthodox, those who entered the priesthood already married.

7. I am indebted to Dr. Ephraim Radner and his *The End of the Church: A Pneumatology of Christian Division in the West* (Grand Rapids: Eerdmans, 1998) for drawing my attention to this passage. The citation from Thomas may be found in *Summa Theologica* (Chicago: Encyclopaedia Britannica, 1952) vol. 22, 646.

own "perfection," namely unreserved self-giving for those put into one's care, even to the point of death. Listen to what Thomas has to say on the role of the bishop, especially in connection with the question of whether or not he can flee persecution:

> . . . in any obligation the chief thing to be considered is the end of the obligation. Now bishops bind themselves to fulfill the pastoral office for the sake of the salvation of their subjects. Consequently, when the salvation of his subjects demands the personal presence of the pastor, the pastor should not withdraw his personal presence from his flock, even in the face of some impending danger to his person, since the good shepherd is bound to lay down his life for the sheep.

Clearly the guiding text here is John 10:1–18 and its contrast between the good shepherd and the hireling. The chief end Thomas has in mind for the bishop as chief pastor is devotion to the flock's salvation even to the point of death. That sense of commitment, "until we are parted by death," is therefore what defines the role of bishop. (It is for this reason that a practice like translation to another diocese was repugnant to him, as it was in the ancient Church, as evidenced by the canons of the Council of Nicaea, since it amounted to something like ecclesiastical no-fault divorce.) The point is that the pastor is bound to the diocesan flock in a manner whose closest analogy is indeed marriage. So for Thomas the bishop's bands are in lieu of marriage, while for Anglicans they are reinforced by the pastor's marriage, but by opposite means each reinforces the symbolic connection.

WHAT SORT OF ANSWER HAVE WE GIVEN?

If this is the sort of symbol, among various symbols, that priesthood is in the community of faith, then we can see why it is difficult to capture in definition. The way things hang together (Col 1:17), the assumption about oath-making that conditions all symbols, are features easily overlooked. And yet they lie at the heart of the nature of a Body (Eph 4:1–4 and following) and of the nature of a covenant. So there is something uniquely powerful and evocative about the priest, though it ought to have nothing to do with his or her own numinous quality in a personal sense. It has to do, rather, with the elusive task of representing the avowed nature of all the Body's symbols as well as the depth and duration of Christ's prior pledge to it. The priest reminds the Body of what lies in, with, and under all the gifts and persons one can observe, that is, the unbreakable promise the Head bestows on His Body, lovingly sealed in His blood, and truly represented in the bread and wine they gather to consume. As a result the priest shows the life of discipleship, of complete self-offering, which is the fitting response to the troth of God.

What we are proposing is a semiotic understanding of the priesthood. We do not understand the role in relation to the power to perform sacred tasks, nor in terms of those functions themselves, but rather in relation to the symbolic meaning the priest holds. He or she is a symbol in a larger field of symbols. The priest has his or her meaning in relation to those whose spiritual lives are ordered by the grace of Christ, who live under the pledge of baptism, etc.

There is a standard distinction made between signs, that point simply and directly, and symbols, that disclose their meaning from within the life experience of the recipient. The discursive text may convey cognitive meaning, while the work of art conveys affective meaning. Each provides its own kind of knowledge. For our present purposes, it suffices to say that the priest in the Church comprises both kinds of knowledge. The priest teaches Scripture, and the priest communicates that same Gospel message as himself or herself a living symbol for the congregation which works affectively and cannot be reduced to content. The impact of the priesthood depends on the consonance of the two. The Word is understood as it is heard cognitively, aesthetically, morally, in suffering, etc., in relation to the whole congregation.

BACK TO OUR QUESTION ONCE AGAIN

Let us return once again to our key question: why does such an understanding of the Church as symbol, and as a result the priest as secondary symbol, conduce to a lifelong priesthood? Why couldn't the reminding and participating be handed off in turns, like household chores? Here the Biblical concept of *dwelling* can be of help to us. The theme runs throughout the Scripture, though, in keeping with God's nature, dwelling is always of a sort that leaves God free and so gracious. The worship of the ark and then the Temple, the promise of the child Emmanuel, the coming Lord whose glory will cover the earth as the waters the sea: God's dwelling with His people is the ongoing hope, fulfilled in an unsurpassable way (Col 1:19), in an openly hidden way, in the incarnation. As a result of the return of the Son to the Father, the Spirit comes to dwell with His people, never more to leave. On the basis of the assurance of this promise, expressing as it does the utter faithfulness of God, Christians can respond with fidelity in their own lives to Christ the Lord, to the spouse to whom they have given their "troth," their promise, to their brother or sister in Christ, and to their neighbor. Because Christ has "remained" or dwelt with us (e.g., John 1:39), we are assured that God will grant us the final rest (Heb 4) of His fully revealed presence in His Kingdom (Rev 20). He has dwelt with us forever, so we are sure that we can "dwell in the house of the Lord forever" (Ps 23:6, KJV).

The priest is a symbol of this one aspect of the hope by which we live. He or she is called to remind the whole Body of the reality of indwelling, of the permanence and duration of that hope. Priests can only be an adequate symbol of this aspect insofar as they bear this symbolic task with their very being, and so for the duration of their life. He or she also reminds all how this assurance permeates the whole of the Body, how it orders the whole, and so cannot be rightly represented by one more function or task.

The life of the priest as a sign of duration does not logically require prolonged cures. It is one's priesthood itself that symbolizes duration, and so being such a symbol does not depend on years of service in one place. Still, it should be noted that the lengths of pastoral placements have been dramatically shortened over the past generation. It would be good to see clergy claiming the monastic tradition of stability, of dwelling in a single "place," for that staying-put was related to dying-to-self, by which we can point to One beyond ourselves. The priest who darts from one assignment to another risks blurring the sign.

3
The Priest as Church in Miniature

BALOKOLE—KEEPING THE FIRE IN THE FIREPLACE

After a promising start, things were not going well for the Anglicans of east Africa in 1935. The missionaries of the Church Missionary Society had prevailed in their struggle against the slave trade and converted a first generation of Christian leaders along the way. Education had progressed by leaps and bounds, the name for a convert in Kiswahili being an *msomi*, "a reader." The first generation of catechists had fanned out to convert the outlying tribes, spearheaded by saints like Apolo Kivebulaya, apostle to the pygmies, who had trekked thousands of miles in obedience to the great commission. But in the intervening years, the Church had been dogged by persistent problems: in Uganda in 1930 as many as 70% of the Christians in the villages could not take communion because their personal lives were irregular, especially in relation to polygamy. Many would lapse back into older idolatrous practices in moments of personal crisis. There were complaints of unfair treatment and racial misunderstandings between native and missionary Christians.[1]

Then something extraordinary happened. An argument between a Rwandan named Nsibambi and a missionary named Joe Church flared up. They confronted one another, talked about their various complaints, confessed them to one another, and found that the power of the Holy Spirit had descended, clearing away the bitterness as well as their vestigial clinging to the old life. Suddenly, as they told their story, others came to "put their sins in the light" and experienced the same joyous relief. They formed a fellowship and started going village to village. The movement, soon to be called the East African Revival, ignited and combusted throughout the region in a matter of months, its participants soon calling themselves the *Balokole*, "the saved." There were good fruits, the power to put aside the old dishonesties and compromises, in order to follow Jesus wholeheartedly. There were also problems, like revivalists sitting in trees outside church to denounce the secret sinners as they walk out of Sunday service, or being tempted to leave the compromised and mixed body to form a pure and separate Church of the saved. They were at times all too ready to say that only they, the Balokole, were saved, the rest of the Church being consigned to be a lumpen mass of complacent damnation. The dramatic change in their lives had been marked by visible shifts in lifestyle:

1. See John V. Taylor's *The Growth of the Church in Buganda: An Attempt at Understanding* (London: SCM, 1958).

abandoning smoking and drinking and the sexual vices that accompanied the latter. But to many these personal changes smacked of puritanical legalism.[2] They were fiercely committed to the truth of the Scripture, but were all too quick to brand the (quite conservative) missionary teachers at the theological college in Mukono as heretics.

In spite of all this, the Balokole remained within the Anglican fold. This was due in large measure to the patient diplomacy of some missionary bishops who were committed to keeping the movement, and the vitality it brought, in the Church. The historical precedents for such a challenge cannot have been lost on those evangelical Anglican bishops. Roughly two centuries earlier, Anglican Church leaders had failed to maintain the renewal movement that would become Methodism within their borders, and so an incalculable opportunity for growth and renewal within the Church was lost. By contrast, the stunning growth of the Anglican Church in east Africa, and hence its burgeoning influence in the wider Anglican Communion, can in large measure be directly traced back to keeping this renewal inside.

As a result of the success in keeping the revival Anglicans within the fold, we find today the anomaly of Churches in Uganda, Tanzania, and Kenya whose episcopal leaders are members of a movement dedicated to the shaking and challenging of the dry officialdom of the established Church. How can they both run the institu-

2. On the moral approach of the Balokole, see Max Alexander Cunningham Warren, *Revival, An Enquiry* (London: SCM, 1954).

tion and challenge it to be renewed? With this question we are brought back to the very roots of the Reformation, where Churches are established by leaders committed to the principle that the Church should be *semper reformanda.* To use more recent language from the charismatic renewal movement, those missionary bishops, and the indigenous bishops who have followed, have been committed to "keeping the fire in the fireplace," keeping the renewal in the structured and inherited Church, and to living with the continuing creative tension created thereby.[3]

THE AGONISTIC LIFE

When we address the question of a theology of the Church, the central experience with which we must come to grips is disappointment. Why does the Church show so little of holiness and so much of the world? Why does so much of its activity seem to have so little to do with proclaiming Jesus or living out our discipleship? How are we to understand the Church so as to take cognizance of these disappointing truths, at the same time we identify the Church with its true goals? What sort of concept of the Church can comprise both our hope and our realism? The question is hardly limited to theologians, but is asked, implicitly, by myriad stoics in the pews each Sunday.

It is in light of these grassroots questions that we can make the best sense of one of the basic decisions in eccle-

3. See Charles E. Hummel, *The Fire In The Fireplace: Contemporary Charismatic Renewal* (Downers Grove, IL: InterVarsity, 1980).

siology. Do we define the Church in terms of its structures, no matter how lively or moribund they may be? Such are most of the classic definitions of the Church—the Church is where the faith of Augsburg is acknowledged, or the Pope has authority, or the threefold ministry in succession is found, etc. By contrast, we might locate the Church wherever gathered Christians are truly doing what the Church is called to do.[4] Does the *ecclesia* come first, or is the true community the *ecclesiola*, the cell of faithfulness within the larger entity?

Attractive as this latter alternative may seem, definitions of the Church in terms of the remnant, the gathered faithful, run into problems. If the true Church is only where holiness happens, then how can we talk meaningfully of a sinful Church, as the Bible often does? What of faith known only to God, buried in the all-too-compromised parish, which John Calvin found even in the corrupt Roman Church of his time? (One thinks of the old joke, I can't join that congregation, it's full of hypocrites—no worry, there's room for one more.) Along the same trajectory is Paul's

4. On this renewal-oriented, "actualist" ecclesiology, Paul Zahl in his *A Short Systematic Theology* (Grand Rapids: Eerdmans, 2000) is eloquent: "Yet we also have to confront the 'facts on the ground' of the crowded, open-straw churches of east Africa, packed and jammed with their Christian multitudes, and the overflowing house churches of China, caught up in a revival beyond numbering . . . . The tornado of God's fervent rush comes and goes through human history. Any geography of Christian church growth will immediately demythologize any tradition we still possess of a standing army of Christian believers and traditions," 89. We would, however, see this as only one side of the dialectic that ecclesiology requires.

insistence that "no one can say 'Jesus is Lord' except by the Holy Spirit" (1 Cor 12:3, NRSV). The implication of this verse is that the Church is found wherever Jesus is named and praised, however compromised those lifting the praises may be. But this too would make things too simple, since it obviously does matter to God if a congregation is morally and spiritually compromised. Where does all this leave us?

We are thrown back on our first question: how does the soundness of the structure of the whole relate to the faithfulness of the remnant? Here we do well to think about a Christian account of the time in which we live. The structures of office, creed, and canon preserve the truth of the Gospel over the long haul, as the Church waits for the consummation; these structures enable the Church to carry on faithfully through the long "not yet" of the Church's life. But the periodic excrescences of renewed life remind us that we live in the time of first fruits of that consummation itself; they are signs of the intrusion of the "already" into our presence. They remind us that the Church should look changed, and show evidences of the Holy Spirit. They are down payments on the future God promises for the Church. At the same time they too are fallible and soon come to show their flaws; often renewal movements decompose in heresy or excess. If the tension between "not yet" and "already" is inevitable short of the Lord's return, we may hazard a guess that there will likewise be no easy choice between the two, between Church as structure and Church as moment. The question of the exact nature of their relationship remains.

The Church is best understood as itself the story of the interaction between its orthodox structures and its movements of renewal. It *is* the tension between the two, like flint striking with sparks of truth. From this perspective, consider the Church's history. In the first period of the Church's life the martyrs were the real elite of the Body, those whose faithful suffering embodied the faithfulness of the Church. One recalls Ignatius of Antioch's claim that only as he felt the lion's jaws about his neck would he be a real Christian. This same era saw the creation of the instruments by which the Church's teaching were preserved: the canon, the creed, the threefold ministry. The structures that defined identity came into being. But even in the Patristic era, the maintenance of these structures was not enough for the integrity of the Church, as we can witness in the struggle over apostasy that led to the Donatist controversy.

After the Constantinian revolution, the very disappearance of the martyrs led to worries that the seriousness of discipleship would be lost, and occasioned the next eruption of renewal within the larger Church, Christian asceticism. The source of the vitality of the medieval Church was in large measure the series of its renewal movements. In the fourth century, in the wake of desert fathers and mothers, we are told that it was hard to find a free cave in Egypt! In the sixth century, the collapse of the Empire coincides with the birth of the Benedictine movement. Its orders, and the next generations of more stringent descendants like the Cluniacs, helped to preserve the faith and gradually expand its reach in the Middle Ages.

Likewise, moral compromise in the Church of the twelfth century was the context for the rise of the mendicant movements, the Dominicans and the Franciscans. To see how renewal often takes place in the Church, the example of the Franciscans is most instructive. Francis's goal was simply obedience to the commanding voice he heard from the cross in the parish Church of Assisi. He set out in utter poverty, not with some more grandiose aim of renewing the wider Church, but simply to build up the dilapidated church of San Damiano, and to care for lepers. In the process he attracted the attention and concern of the Papacy, to whose authority he humbly submitted himself. Yet his personal sanctity, and the dramatically simple presentation of the Gospel his life represented, served to challenge and transform the Church. Francis embodied the fruitful tension between obedience to the structures of tradition and the fire of sanctity and renewal. To be sure, the Franciscans, too, underwent change and suffered moral compromise. By the time of Francis's death, they were one of the wealthiest orders in Europe! In light of this longer-term pattern of rise and fall, the value of the undergirding structures is clear. A more demanding call to Gospel obedience, a sodality or society within the larger Church formed to answer this call, and a more diffuse and prolonged effect on the Church as a whole: that is the pattern of Franciscanism, and of many other renewal movements as well.

The Reformation seems the sharpest counter-example, since the wider communion surrounding the renewal movement was not preserved. Yet Martin Luther's original intention was to spark a movement of renewal in the Church by greater attention to the Word of God, in a manner reminiscent of the lay movement called the *devotio moderna*. Events in the heightened conflict made this impossible.[5] This vision of Lutheranism as in truth an extended renewal movement within catholic Christendom has been reclaimed in modern ecumenical efforts.

At the dawn of the modern era, on both sides of the divide between Catholics and Protestants, we see the emergence of the missionary movement. The Society of Jesus of the sixteenth century was a highly disciplined order loyal to the Catholic structure and committed to its strengthening. They were among the most innovative and courageous examples of the worldwide Christian mission. Nineteenth-century Africa is transformed by groups like the Catholic White Fathers, on the one hand, and the evangelical Anglican Church Missionary Society, on the other. Their work of bringing the Gospel, translating the necessary languages, and planting Churches which could be locally spread, has led to the contemporary explosion in numbers of members among Third World Churches. But here again, the transformation of the global Church was not the goal, but rather a more radical response to the Great Imperative, heard anew.

Here the example of the Church Missionary Society is illustrative. The late eighteenth-century Church of England

5. A number of modern Lutheran scholars have seen a more "Catholic" Luther, and have wished to think of Lutheranism throughout its history as a movement of reform within Catholicism.

was, by most accounts, moribund, but the founders of the CMS did not aim at its reform. They aimed simply to bring the Gospel to those who had not heard it. In the accomplishment of this task they remained resolutely the *Church* Missionary Society, loyal to their mother Church and careful to include bishops on their governing board. But their fervor for evangelism could not have been more different than their peers, and that fervor changed the face of the world Church a century later.

Those founders of the CMS, men and women like Charles Simeon, Hanah More, and Henry Venn, were evangelicals, members of a wider movement of renewal in personal devotion that began with the Pietists themselves in eighteenth-century Europe. The Pietists themselves did not imagine they were beginning a new Church, but rather founding *ecclesiolae*, mini-Church bodies, within the larger Church. Likewise even to the time of his death John Wesley, in part under pietist influence, understood his ministry of preaching and the promotion of the class meetings as a force for renewal within the Anglican Church. So, too, in characters like Simeon and Venn we see the fruitful use of a voluntary society, loyal to the Church but moving freely within it. This same strategy, using what we would today call a "para-Church organization," demonstrates once again the creative friction between macro-Church structures and micro-renewal efforts, for such organizations are in and for the Church, but not precisely of it structurally.[6] Thus they

6. Similarly the theological college or seminary, in most cases, has this same loyal but anomalous lodging within ecclesial life.

are able to work in the interstices of the structure without direct conflict with it.

Something similar may be found in most parish Churches, where a lively women's group, men's prayer breakfast, or youth movement serves as the catalyst for new life in the Church as a whole. Martin Thornton turned this observation into a whole theory of parish leadership around the concept of the remnant.[7] In the latter half of the twentieth century perhaps the most instructive lesson in the-few-for-the many has been the charismatic movement that swept across a number of mainline Churches. Where it has been wisely guided it has brought the fruitful tension that leads to growth and new life. But where either Church leaders or charismatic members have lost sight of the vision of Church as narrative of structure in renewal, the result has been divisiveness and suppression.

In our first argument we reflected the relationship between being in orders as a priest, and the ordering of truth to Christ. In the second argument the priest underlines the order of oath-making and keeping for all the symbol-members of the Body. In the case of our third argument, we also find a new sense of "order." We have argued that the Church is the tension-laden relationship between structure and movements of renewal, the latter represented in many cases by missionary or ascetical orders. Priests find themselves at the intersection of warp and woof. They are servants of the Church and so representatives of its tra-

7 See, e.g., Martin Thorton, *Pastoral Theology: A Reorientation* (London: SPCK, 1956).

ditional structures. But they themselves ought also to be a kind of order, a "society of Jesus," as they point to His Lordship and its gracious action.

But how are they to be both at the same time? What form does this order take at the present moment in the Church? How do loyalty and renewal relate to one another? We cannot provide a formulaic answer, for to be a priest is to work out with one's very life an answer to this question. This straitening, this bind, is no accident, but embedded in the very ordered life to which he or she as priest is bound. The priest acts this out and so displays it for all fellow Christians, and in doing so is a symbol of the very nature of the Church. More pointedly and poignantly, we may ask what is the priest to do when the bishop for whom he or she serves seems to contradict the very teachings.[8] Here the straitening, by which the priest plays out in his or her own career, parish leadership, and thinking, expresses itself in a narration of submission and witness, in suffering and personal loss. In his or her own life the priest comes to bear the marks of the Church that sojourns between the times.

Once again we must ask why this account of ordained ministry requires indelibility. This, our third argument, might be termed "agonistic," for it sees the unavoidable tension or struggle between institution and renewal, to be built into the calling. In the priest's life dedication to the Church in all its concreteness, and the renewal for which Christ summons us to follow and die, collide. We must

8. See Ephraim Radner's essay "Bad Bishops," in *Hope Among the Fragments* (Grand Rapids: Brazos, 2004) 177–96.

struggle with this twofold calling "until we are parted" from it "by death." But to be a priest for a season would relieve the very dramatic tension which the priest must display and under which he or she must prove faithful. She or he could serve until such time as the calling became uncomfortable, and then could find something more congenial. Then the calling would cease to be the twofold yoke it is meant to be. The priest is called to a life with no exit, no ready resolution, unless one re-conceives one's life radically by looking away to Christ for the only sort of resolution possible.

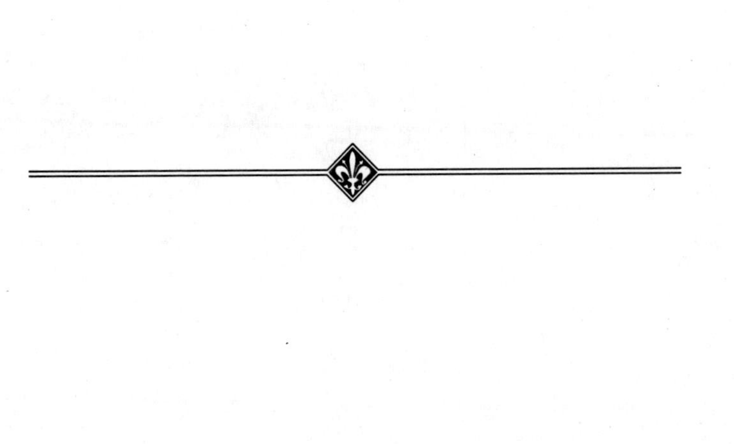

4
So What?

We have offered three answers to the question about indelible orders, three accounts of the nature of the priesthood itself which amount to answers about the nature of the Church. It is fair to wonder what the ministerial world we live in would look like if such views were widely adopted. What are the implications of these three visions? Do they have a practical "cash-out" that changes the way we train future priests, the way we think about the culture's advice to us, or the way we organize our parish lives? It is to these questions of application that we must now turn.

BEYOND ZERO SUM

All of our arguments present a symbolic or iconic understanding of priesthood. Throughout, we have thought about priesthood from an angle quite different from that of power. So the first clear implication of priesthood, properly understood, is that it must not be thought of over against, or in competition with, the prerogatives of the laity. It is for the laity, both practically and symbolic, that priests serve in the Church.

The astute observer of parishes and their vitality can confirm this point. For the congregations with the strongest lay leaders exercising the widest array of gifts, are those with clergy who are clearest about who they are and what they are. One could go so far as to say that such clergy are a condition of the possibility of a strong laity.

If we think of the ordained and the laity in this non-"zero-sum," mutually conditioning manner, then we leave behind the competing claims of each to power or control. Ideally, relations between the two are so recast that the nature and "feel" of parish conflict could be ameliorated as well. Secular models derived from business or politics, assumed in an unspoken way, can be transformed. Most importantly, the relationship is placed on a self-consciously theological footing.

THEOLOGICAL SPINE

In our first account of the priesthood, in which he or she points to the Word, the role of exegete, of Christian rabbi, is paramount. He or she must witness "against the grain" of cultural assumptions. In the second account, the priest serves as a sign of the promissory, avowed nature of the Christian life. The third account focuses on the renewing remnant within and for the Church as a whole, while they remain loyal to the Church in which they are in orders. Here too they need a broader perspective than is common.

What kind of theological education is required for the formation, by the grace of God, of clergy who fit this profile? We will continue to work in threes, and will offer three qualities of theological education which exemplifies this vision of the ordained.

First of all, the theological education required is one that is deeply traditional in the best sense. The student must see himself or herself as apprenticed to a guild of thought and practice which has preceded them and whose language they must learn. This tradition will have at this center the great doctrines of faith: the Trinity, the incarnation, the atonement, justification, all of which articulate in their different ways the Lordship of Jesus Christ. Such theological education must be, in short, self-consciously orthodox.[1] This must serve, of course, as a rule to guide the reading of Scripture, to which the lion's share of time in seminary should be devoted. At a practical level, this requires some expression in the curriculum and community life of recent efforts[2] to break down the wall of division between the theological disciplines. To read the whole Bible by the rule of faith with an eye to the traditional and sacramental practices of the Church: this is the sense in which theological education's holy grail, integration, should be pursued. We may think of a highly traditional education in Scripture

1. There is a place here for the use of the "Great Books" which require an immediate engagement with the tradition and the asking of good questions of the text.

2. We have in mind here recent efforts at "theological exegesis" spearheaded by thinkers like Oden and Reno.

and doctrine as a kind of spine giving shape to the priestly life and actually making pastoral flexibility possible.[3]

This kind of education aims, secondly, to widen the imagination of the student, so that the Church to which he or she is ordained includes the cloud of witnesses who have preceded and our grandchildren in the faith, as well as Christians to the very ends of the earth. It should include the ecumenical and devotional range of Christian possibilities. Only as students are shown, visually or in the mind's eye, a much wider range of what the Church can be can they withstand the tyranny of cultural fad and obsession. The missionary too, who can go into a place seemingly unpromising or un-evangelized, lives from a vision of the much wider communion of which he or she is still a part, and of the fruit that may only be seen by their successors. The balancing of immediate loyalty and the possibility of renewal which our third account emphasized is actually a single loyalty to the Church more expansively understood. Concretely in the life of a school this wider imagination might come from an international student or the visit of a long-term missionary, a placement in a charismatic parish, or the study of Patristic liturgy.

At the same time, ordinands must have the capacity for a deep attachment and empathy for the actual communities before them. They must have a sense that God has given these very Christians into their care. This must be accompanied by a theology of the Church in its concrete-

3. See my inaugural address as Principal of Wycliffe College in the fall issue, 1999, of the journal of the Toronto School of Theology.

ness, and its flaws, as the place where God can and does convey his message of grace: "for we have this treasure in clay pots . . ." In the end this attachment depends upon virtues like charity,[4] humility, and patience. But it can surely be enhanced by effective lay work before seminary, and by a serious and selective program of mentorship or apprenticeship in parishes. Seminaries would do better to work with the few who are truly exemplars in this regard, however difficult this may be logistically.

It is easy to fault theological education today, but one must appreciate the myriad pressures under which programs exist. They are chronically underfunded. They sometimes receive mandates from Church structures which must be added to already overloaded curricula. In many cases clergy no longer go out to curacies (assistantships) but often must immediately run their own shows. Students complain about the hardships of uprooting and want more short-term or on-line options and shorter residential stays. Leaders of struggling denominations want education that is more practical and results-oriented. We are calling for a kind of education which is more traditional and against-the-grain. Here theological education ought to be allied with the liberal arts in arguing that what is not oriented immediately to practicality and results will in the long run, ironically, prove to be so.

4. One might in fact see our three points about theological education as corresponding to the theological virtues of faith, hope, and love.

Thidly, theological education needs, quite simply, to be more devotionally intense. Daily office, prayer group, ruled disciplines of private prayer, the retrieval of self-examination and preparation for communion: we need a more rigorous spiritual life. In general the Church has become "softer" and more lax in the last two generations, in keeping with a feature of the culture as a whole.[5] If seminaries are to be seedbeds, their atmospheres, in spite of the risks, should more resemble hot-houses.

INDELIBLY THREEFOLD?

Each of the arguments answers the more general question about the nature of the Church on the way to answering the more specific question about indelible orders. By backing up and addressing the more basic issue of ordered ministry per se first, we have sought to provide evangelical reasons for this feature of catholic tradition. But how does indelibility pertain to each of the traditional threefold ministries? For it is as bishops, priests, and deacons that the ordained are sealed for life. This too is a given practice, a fact, with its own murky origins. If a case for indelibility can be made, then perhaps it can help to make sense of the form orders have taken in the historic Church. Can we, then, give a plausible reason specifically for the threefold indelible ministry?

5. See for example Michael Barone, *Hard America, Soft America: Competition vs. Coddling and the Battle for the Nation's Future* (New York: Crown Forum, 2004).

We can again lay out in brief the historical facts, as one lays out an obstacle course to make the run more challenging. First, as we have already stated, there is no clarity whether bishops grew out of a primordial priesthood, or vice versa. (Another possibility is that the answers differ in different sees of the early Church). Secondly, we find in Ignatius of Antioch a rich variety of typological correspondences (between the bishop and the Father, the presbyter and the apostles, etc.) but little consistency. Thirdly, while we already see the notion of three distinct orders in the early 2nd century with St. Ignatius, the notion of sequential orders, of the *cursus honorum*, only emerged later, under the cultural influence of the Roman civil service.[6] This does not mean that the patristic evidence is not useful. But at the same time this plasticity frees us for a creative construal of the given practice.

Consider the following description of the Church: *Hiddenly present in the Church, Christ speaks His promise, as Word and sacrament, across time and space until He returns.* What is comprised in such a definition of the Church? Christ is present in the Church, of this we can be sure and from this we can take comfort. But this presence is always hidden, veiled, for the Church is yet a sinful creature, slothful, disobedient. It not only sits at supper with Him, it also walks along unable to see who walks beside it. Secondly, as we saw in our second argument, the Church is a promis-

6. The definitive work on the *cursus honorum* is John St. H. Gibaut, *The Cursus Honorum: A Study of Origins and Evolution of Sequential Ordination* (New York: Lang, 2000).

sory reality. Christ promises to be present with us "to the end of the age" (Matt 28:20, NRSV). He makes a promise of eternal life to us, by which we can live, but for which we must still hope. Thirdly, Christ makes this promise in and to the Church as the Church engages in its distinctive, "dominical" acts—it preaches the word, it baptizes disciples, it celebrates the supper of His body and blood. The promise is something Christ does, expressed characteristically in acts that the Church does. So the believer may understand every liturgy to be Christ reaching out to address and embrace His people. Fourth and finally, for all its divisions and discords, the Church is best understood as one, long, sustained, consistent utterance of that promise across time and space. From the time of His ascension, until His coming again, in a plethora of places, occasions, and manner, Christ utters His promise to the Church. The action is one, only because the Actor is one and the same, "yesterday and today and forever" (Heb 13:8, NRSV).

If we take the definition of the Church's purpose stated above, how then would we conceive of the threefold, indelible, ordained ministry? What feature of this one purpose does each order represent? Again, since the practice precedes the explanation, a number of answers could conceivably be given, but the following suits well the preceding definition. The *deacon* highlights the humble and serving nature of the ministry, its lowliness in this "clay pot" condition in which the Church finds itself. He or she is an icon of the *hiddenness* of the open secret that is the Gospel. As such he or she will be a sign of contradiction for all presumption, prestige, and worldly power wielded by the Church. It ought to serve here in the kind of self-deflating role discussed in our first argument. The *priest* is the typical president in today's ordinary parish, and as such lives out in his or her daily life the centrality of the Word and sacraments as the means of salvation to ordinary parishioners. They are the ones who stand at the center of Eucharistic communities (in the same sense that Ignatius used for the second century bishop), and so live out their indelible vocations as signs of the *irrevocably promissory nature of the means of salvation.* We have seen in the first argument that this "signing" will involve reminding a community that the Word, heard and seen, is at the center, and not a multitude of other worldly pursuits. Finally, the *bishop* is the sign of the *continuity* of the Church, the endurance of the Gospel across time, space, and indeed across the vagaries of the eccentric ideas of certain eras and Churches. Here too the bishop will be required at times to exercise a ministry of resisting what is peculiar and errant in his or her own diocese, in short, to resist at times the excessively local views of the very tribe for whom he is sworn to care. The three ministries together convey well the definition we have offered.

How does such a unified vision of the Church, symbolized in the threefold ministry, comport with indelibility? The Church may be seen as a single promissory ministry, extended over time. Lifelongness in the three, complementary orders corresponds to this patient, enduring quality of the Church awaiting Christ's return.

LEADERSHIP: DESPOILING THE EGYPTIANS

Two generations ago we expected clergy to understand themselves as "helping professionals," and one generation ago they were to be "servants."[7] Today clergy need to be "leaders": but what does this mean, and what does preoccupation with the term bespeak about a theology of the ordained?

This trend among the ordained cannot be separated from secular interest in leadership, in corporations as well as non-profits, and so our question can only be answered as we pay attention to this wider context for the term. What does the term mean to authors across disciplines?

The leader is first of all one who has a vision for the institution, and can convey it to others. Bill Hybels of the vastly successful Willowcreek Church has defined "vision" as "a picture of the future that produces passion." Here the worry is that the head of the institution may be mired in immediate problems, confused as to the direction to be taken, or discouraged by the paucity of resources for the task. The emphasis on vision seeks to put first things first, to look at the big picture, to remind employees why they came in the first place, to offer a goal that others can share, etc.

The pursuit of a vision must, secondly, address the need for constant change. This point is in part the product of the volatile and fiercely competitive business scene in today's global marketplace. Corporations need to recreate

7. See for an example among many, Robert K. Greenleaf, *The Servant as Leader* (Indianapolis: Greenleaf, 1991).

themselves repeatedly as their markets and products shift. "Major changes are more and more necessary to survive and compete effectively in this [business] environment. More change always demands more leadership."[8] This emphasis on change has entrenched itself as a cultural good, such that politicians can run on slogans like "change is good" or "embrace change." Thus the leader is the one who can bring about fruitful change, manage its distresses, and allay its attendant anxieties.

To accomplish this, the leader must, thirdly, balance the promotion of energetic and creative chaos with the fostering of supportive and nurturing environment. The former goal owes a debt to the cultural ideal of the entrepreneur, while the latter borrows from the psychological, therapeutic realm. Both together aim to compensate for the deficits which are perceived to exist in the manager, perhaps the defining role in our increasingly bureaucratized culture.[9] As to the former goal, the leader allows the staff to feel realistic "distress," while he or she protects internal criticism, what one article on business leadership called "protecting voices of leadership from below."[10] On

8. See John Kotter, "What Leaders Really Do," in *On Leadership*, Harvard Business Review Paperback Series (Boston: Harvard Business School Press, 1998) 37–60.

9. On the managerial in modernity see Alasdair MacIntyre, *After Virtue: A Study in Moral Theory*, 2d ed. (Notre Dame: University of Notre Dame Press, 1984) 26–27, 30–32, 74–78, and 85–87.

10. Ronald Heifetz and Donald Laurie in *On Leadership*, Harvard Business Review Paperback Series (Boston: Harvard Business School Press, 1998) 185.

the other side of the ledger, the leader must act as a mentor who can "entrust emerging leaders with responsibility."[11] With respect to both goals, the leadership watchword of our time is surely "empowerment."

The aforementioned features of leadership involve relations with others, but the literature of leadership has spent equal time attending to the personal, moral features of the leader himself or herself. Such literature enumerates, fourthly, the requisite virtues of the leader. One author on the art of managing people contends that "great management involves courage and tenacity. It closely resembles heroism."[12] The most commonly cited qualities are perseverance, integrity, honesty, even tenderness toward subordinates. Max De Pree speaks of the managerial need to delegate tasks in a manner reminiscent of the Christian literature of asceticism: "while good delegation requires a form of dying, it is also the only way for leaders to stay alive."[13] The emphasis on servanthood, assuming as it does humility, has endured as well. One definition of the leader's quality of self-abnegation is the ability to focus, not on oneself, but rather on the institution and its mission. One leads precisely as one pays no attention to one's own leadership.[14]

11. Bill Hybels, *Courageous Leadership* (Grand Rapids: Zondervan, 2002) chapter 6.

12. See Thomas Teal's article in *On Leadership*, Harvard Business Review Paperback Series (Boston: Harvard Business School Press, 1998) 147ff.

13. See Max De Pree's *Leadership Jazz* (New York: Dell, 1993) 158.

14. De Pree, *Leadership Jazz*, 28.

In large measure the literature of leadership has in the business realm sought to answer the charge that management is an impersonal, objectifying process of seeing humans as systems and assets: one may respond that this literature doth protest too much! (The Church has borrowed many of these notions, though it may not have had the very bottom-line hard-headedness they were designed to overcome.) Leadership talk is trying to keep the efficiency of business, and give it a human face. To this end, it tries, fifthly, to see the dimensions of human society that are not patent of manipulation and technique, the symbolic, the interpersonal, the moral, the value-laden.[15] We will delineate the specific emphases of this literature of efficient yet humanized leadership.

Consider the following example of the application of leadership talk to the Church which displays all these salient features. *Church Leadership* by Lovett Weems presents a more liberal point of view than the Church growth movement represents, but this changes little, since all such Christian authors depend so heavily on their secular antecedents. Weems's work is subtitled "Vision, Team, Culture, and Integrity." Under "Team" he speaks of the means by which colleagues are empowered, involved, and challenged, our second point. Under "Integrity" he speaks of the virtues necessary for the leader. By "Culture" he means the features of a working society that elude normal business analysis, the symbolic and the ritual. He notes (tellingly for our

15. The irony is of course that the self-help book by its nature offers a technique.

purposes) that any Church culture will generate standard symbolic roles to communicate the true nature of its common life.[16]

This strong echo of our own, more theological argument, should give us the tip we need to understand the significance of the literature of leadership. The Church is borrowing back its own patrimony, for the key words in this literature were first borrowed from the Church: vision, mission statement, empowerment, gifts, promise, prophetic critique, the pastoral, mentoring, virtues. Leadership books would have us borrow such categories from the managers at Pepsi or GM, but they got the words originally from us! The Church, forgetful of its own tradition, comes to hear it again as if it were something alien and new.[17]

Clergy find the literature of leadership helpful. But it would prove truly fruitful if it were replanted in the richer spiritual and theological soil from which it came. "Vision," "mission," "culture," "virtues": the key terms are strangely abstract and formal, and they leave the pastor with the task

16. Lovett H. Weems, *Church Leadership: Vision, Team, Culture, Integrity* (Nashville: Abingdon, 1993) 111–12.

17. Another obvious example of this process of forgetting and reappropriating is the phenomenon of Alcoholics Anonymous. The language of surrender and powerlessness to change on one's own, of the need of grace and confidence in its empowerment, reverberate with the echoes of the language of Christian conversion. Yet the movement has shorn its references to Christ. It dwells in the very basements where the original language of grace was spoken, though now it is sometimes forgotten. While AA seemed to offer a new influence on the Church, it actually was another case of the Church borrowing from itself.

of figuring out what the vision is to be, what sort of culture ought to be inculcated. This is just what we would expect in a do-it-yourself, voluntarist society which has spawned the confusion about the pastoral role in the first place. Helpful as they may be, leadership books as self-help literature are emblematic of a profession cut loose from its moorings, its members left to improvise a strategy and a market in each locale they find themselves. Their work does indeed require "Leadership Jazz."[18] This leadership is symptomatic of the breakdown in a sense of theological tradition occasioning the very need for such books.

The categories of the literature of leadership are helpful, and pastors mired in the minutiae of stressful lives would do well to organize their efforts around them. But the content of the vision does not require invention, nor does it benefit from reinvention every time the rectorship changes hands. The vision is provided by close attention to Scripture, read in light of the Creeds. The mission is to preach the Gospel, let your lights so shine, to celebrate the sacraments, to practice the spiritual disciplines. To these ends the virtues required are spelled out in the exhortations of St. Paul. In other words, the substance to which the literature reorients pastors is provided by the classical tradition of mere Christianity which became occluded when such terms became detached. These are not devised, but received with gratitude and submission.

The question of how to relate the literature of leadership to the Christian theological tradition proper is an

18. Hence the title of De Pree's book.

example of the larger question of "inculturation." Valuable insights can be found in this literature, but they need to be "ordered" to the ends found in the Christian tradition proper. Priests making use of such a literature are themselves a prime example of a process of appropriation, of "despoiling the Egyptians." The priest becomes a model of the borrowing, discarding, subordinating, and rearranging that inculturation requires. Yes, the pastor can learn from the businessperson, the child of Mammon, about studying a market, segmenting it, and positioning his or her evangelistic efforts within it. The trick is to make sure that the ethos of the Gospel assimilates these tools, and is not assimilated by them. A nearby Church moves to "open communion" to win its market, or softpedals the atonement as unappealing, or comes to think of members as customers, and the tradition is being despoiled rather than despoiling.

Let us relate this reclaimed literature to our own argument about the ordained ministry. Clergy are an order dedicated to the vision of Christ's Lordship over the Church. This will at times involve what we normally think of as organizational leadership, but it will also require challenging the community as a counter-sign when it seeks to rely upon its own resources in the pursuit of its own preoccupations. Sometimes the priest will resemble the leader as described in the literature, though he or she will also have moments of leading in a contrarian way. The symbolic dimension of the role, recognized in passing in the literature of leadership, will prove to be far more extensive and deep than there imagined.

STRESSING PRIESTHOOD

Terms like "burn-out" and "self-care" are spoken today as frequently in clergy circles as "lectionary" or "salvation." We hear alarming statistics about clergy who are succumbing to the effects of stress on their ministries. Though it is hard to be sure, given that we have little data from earlier eras, it would seem that these acute difficulties are related to the contemporary changes in the nature of the pastor's role and the position of the Church in society.

The term "burnout" is used for several sorts of phenomena. Some clergy suffer from a severe syndrome, known and documented in other helping professions, which bears similarities to the effects after trauma.[19] In most cases the term is used for a more diffused sense of listlessness, discouragement, or anger. There may of course be personal factors at work which are quite unrelated to the parish or theology. Still there are certain identifiable and recurring factors. William Willimon has offered a clear and concise account of these factors, which, taken together, comprise a composite picture of clergy burnout. Some of the reasons he cites are endemic to working in a particular religious community over time: repetitive tasks, vague job descriptions, and the same people year after year. But this could be said of many jobs outside the religious sector. Willimon also cites the lack of closure or a sense of completion of tasks, but this has been cited in management studies as a ubiquitous problem in modern society. Other, more telling

19. See G. Lloyd Rediger, *Coping With Clergy Burnout* (Valley Forge, PA: Judson, 1982) chapter 1.

problems pertain in particular to the predicament of the Church as it is migrates to the margins of society: increased discouragement as numbers fall, and a large number of parishioners who are needy in their emotions and confused in their motives. Finally he emphasizes the burden of the *persona* of the priest, from which they may feel distant or alienated.[20] Willimon's list will doubtless sound familiar to many readers.

It has become a truism to talk of our Church's entry into a "post-Christendom" era, though in some senses this took place half a millennium ago, and in others it has only begun to occur. But assuming at least its partial truth, we may ask what this assertion means. The plight of the clergy may indeed be one of the most concrete expressions of this hard reality. They are like the canaries lowered into the post-Christian mineshaft, for they feel most directly the discouragement of decline, the scurrying about of parishes and denominations in search of social approval, and the confused appropriation of the consumer standards of the culture. Clergy stress and burnout are the somatizations, as it were, of the Church's post-Christendom plight.

It is in this light that we can see most clearly the root cause of these conditions. John Sanford pointed out a full generation ago[21] that what is commonly called burnout really derives from a lack of meaning. More recent and

20. William H. Willimon, *Clergy and Laity Burnout*, Creative Leadership Series (Nashville: Abingdon, 1989) 58.

21. See John A. Sanford, *Ministry Burnout* (New York: Paulist, 1982).

detailed studies, such as the Cornerstone Project of the Episcopal Church Foundation, have confirmed the widespread inability of clergy to articulate what priests should themselves be or what they should be doing.[22] While the other problems are real enough, they have intertwined with them a perplexity that is theological and spiritual at its heart, and relates directly to the concerns of an essay like this one.

Such a problem cannot ultimately find a satisfactory answer by means of psychology, anthropology, or sociology alone. For this reason a theologian like Urban Holmes could see the insufficiency of the Clinical Pastoral Education model to answer this crisis of meaning, but had only a different social scientific gruel to offer for this hunger. Likewise an influential book like Loren Mead's *The Once and Future Church* could identify post-Christendom marginalization as the central issue, but could not offer normative help about what the Church or its pastors ought now to espouse.[23] In both cases, and many others, the theological liberalism in question ruled out more normative and substantive claims rooted in the tradition. They could see the answer from afar but could not reach it.

22. As reported by the Rev. Dr. Leander Harding in "The Power and Dignity of the Priesthood," *Sewanee Theological Review* 43 (2000). Another example is a recent study in Canada by Dr. Andrew Irvine that found identity confusion to be at the root of much clergy stress.

23. Loren Mead, *The Once and Future Church: Reinventing the Congregation for a New Mission Frontier* (Washington, DC: Alban Institute, 1991).

The solutions usually offered for clergy burnout are valid enough in their own rights: to maintain a balance in one's life, to stay healthy, to be quiet each day, to have a hobby, etc. All fall under the rubric of "wholeness,"[24] which has held the field for a full generation. But if the problem is a sense of meaninglessness in the clergy role itself, then these answer are patently insufficient.

ADDRESSING CLERGY IDENTITY

The priest is, first of all, a member of the true order of Jesus, with the clear task of pointing the congregation away from itself and toward Him. While all the discouragements of parish conflict, cultural marginality, pastoral stress, and the unending round of work may remain, the priest has what he or she most keenly needs, a clearer sense of identity. Furthermore that identity depends neither on external cultural, nor internal psychological affirmation. The priest lives under spiritual disciplines, and within a theological tradition, and has inner resources that can withstand long stretches in a foreign land. Unlike our contemporaries in our culture, he or she is not making it up as one goes along. This identity is rooted in those disciplines and that tradition, and so it has a definite and normative content.

24. Two that are as helpful as any are Donald R. Hands and Wayne L. Fehr, *Spiritual Wholeness for Clergy: A New Psychology of Intimacy with God, Self, and Others* (New York: Alban Institute, 1993), and Roy M. Oswald, *Clergy Self-Care: Finding a Balance for Effective Ministry* (Washington, DC: Alban Institute, 1991).

Secondly, the priest can withstand the gales of stress because he or she is tethered.[25] His or her vocation depends on the prior promise of Christ, and on the responding troth pledged in ordination. Here one may recall the great wedding sermon of Dietrich Bonhoeffer, where he tells his niece that her and her fiancé's wedding does not depend on the love she feels, but rather their loving relationship depends on the wedding itself, or rather the covenant contained therein.[26] Likewise the promise found in the ordination service, first by God, then by the ordinand, sustains and maintains the clergy through all that he or she may face. They are after all to be signs of endurance, not of success or even good spirits. But it turns out that this sense of secure tethering does in fact conduce to just such success. As with the married, the priest finds new and unexpected depths of freedom and creativity given by the Holy Spirit emerging from that constraining promise.

Thirdly, the priest comes to understand the tension between movements of renewal and structures of authority to lie at the heart of the calling, instead of finding it to be some dysfunctional aberration. Amidst this tension, priests understand themselves to be contributing downpayments of hope within the Church, like Jeremiah buying the land

25. Using a rock-climbing metaphor, Eugene H. Peterson in *The Unnecessary Pastor: Rediscovering the Call* (Grand Rapids: Eerdmans, 2000) makes the point this way: "vows are pegs, protecting against moods and weather, miscalculation and fatigue," 13. The book is co-authored by Marva J. Dawn and edited by Peter Santucci.

26. See Dietrich Bonhoeffer, *Letters and Papers from Prison* (New York: Macmillan, 1972) 41–55.

at Anathoth in the dark days of the exile (Jer 32:9–15). The priest indwelling the theological tradition sees himself or herself as part of something vaster than one's stresses, namely the cloud of witnesses through the centuries. As a sign of the promise the priest is reminded that he or she is part of a wide community, with its own deep, subterranean life of the Spirit. Finally, as a sign of loyal renewal he or she is reminded of the Church catholic throughout the world, as well as the Church of our grandchildren for whom we are stewards. This seeing of the wider vista is central to the encouragement that a strong sense of a priest's theological identity can offer.

Nowhere is the priest promised that a strong and sound theological identity will guarantee success. At the same time, our Lord tells us to seek the Kingdom and righteousness, and everything else would be given to us as well. We do not hold a theological identity because it works according to Church growth principles—that would succumb to the very functionalism and pragmatism our culture is so prone to. At the same time, clarity of priestly identity may, in addition, offer the clarity of teaching that does tend to strengthen congregations in our time.

But aren't we simply talking about the re-imposition of clerical authoritarianism? Might the loss of such clericalism not be the real reason for clerical identity confusion? And isn't its return too high a price to pay for the resolution of clergy stress? Aren't we in danger of valorizing clerical rigidity? Here we should recall our discussion of authority and its clear distinction from the coercion associated with authoritarianism. Power is exercised in any system, and where authority is lacking power will be wielded by means of manipulation. By contrast our first argument imagines authority as legitimate only as it points on to the true Bearer of authority. Our second argument conceives of the power of the ordained sign only as it highlights the other signs, and our third argument includes themes of obedience and a minority committed to future renewal. In each case the imagined clerical power is buffered or diverted in some fashion.

As the literature of clergy stress highlights, however, a tyrannous clergy is hardly our besetting problem (in spite of some polemics one occasionally reads, for example in some of the literature of total ministry). Laity suffer far more from a confused and demoralized clergy, whose lack of vision in fact impairs the possibility of a strong ministry of the laity. And where clericalism does exist, it is more likely to be the result of too diffuse a sense of clerical identity than too strong an account. Parishes where lay ministries flourish know the truth (with which we began this chapter) that strong clergy who have the spiritual authority which grows from a clear identity conduce to robust lay involvement.

HOW SALT?

Let us return where we began and offer a summation of our argument as a whole. We will do this in the form of a word of explanation about our somewhat cryptic title! So what *does* it mean to "be salt?" We began by citing some of the common and yet unhelpful antinomies in discussions about ordained ministry: a functional vs. an ontological understanding, a lay-oriented vs. a clerically oriented emphasis, the priest *in persona Christi* vs. the priest *in persona ecclesiae*. Throughout this essay we have had a covert interest in subverting these alternatives as we offered our own answer. Quite simply, a sound understanding of the priesthood moves beyond these "either/ors" and recasts the questions.

The New Testament passages[27] about being salt are clearly addressed to the whole community of disciples of Jesus, not a smaller coterie of leaders. The definitive passage is Matt 5:13 (NRSV), "you are the salt of the earth," where Jesus addresses the disciples and tells them that they are to stand in this relationship to the world around them. He goes on to tell them that if they lose this quality they will be useless, for they will be indistinguishable from their environment. Clearly the *Church* is to be salt. Priests, in "being salt," take up the identity that is already theirs as members of the people of God, but in a new way.

This statement is of course part of the Sermon on the Mount, where Jesus presents the New Torah that He brings and is. "Be salt" is, on the one hand, a command from Jesus. On the other hand, the disciples "are salt" with respect to another party to whom they owe a witness. What can we

27. The other passage is Col 4:6, "let your speech be seasoned with salt," and exhorts all Christians to speak in a way that both shows their message to be distinct and winsome. Here salt, due perhaps to its value in the ancient world, is associated with wisdom.

learn from this? One can only "be salt" in relation to two parties, the One who commands, Jesus, and the audience to and for whom one is salt. Saltiness is on the one hand a status bestowed, and on the other hand a relationship lived out. Saltiness is not a possession one can have by one's self. Furthermore, saltiness as Jesus commands it defies the contrast between being and function. It is clearly something they are to *be*, and yet to be salt inherently implies rendering certain services for another. Salt preserves; salt adds zest or flavor. Still, salt does these by what it is for them. The metaphor and the dominical saying on which it is founded seem well to suit the concept of being a "sign for," which takes into itself both sides of the being/doing dichotomy.

Any understanding of the priesthood will then have to take into account three parties, Christ, priest, people of God (and implied therein is a fourth to whom the people are salt, namely the world!). "Priest" is inherently a relational word, for one is a priest *of* Christ and *for* the Church. We have worked this out by describing the priest as the one who empties his or her own claim so as to represent *the Church to itself* as the one who is itself only as it is *pointed to Christ* (so our first argument).

Salt preserves and flavors. Our first argument emphasized the former by means of the role of the priest as the one who guards the Christocentric nature of the Word we have for the world. Our third argument emphasized the latter, for the movement of renewal which the priest encourages makes Gospel tangible and attractive. But what both share, and what lies at the heart of the symbol of salt, is the distinctiveness of the Church over against whatever culture we find ourselves in, over against whatever band of Gentiles are our neighbors. In this generation a chorus of theological voices have been raised to reassert this distinctiveness with a variety of nuances.[28] At the level of ecclesial structure and practice, the priesthood, the salt that preserves and flavors, should be sympathetic to distinctiveness. As we have argued, this makes priests "leaders," but in a very particular way which the culture may find uncomfortable.

But what does salt have to say about indelibility? Salt is required in order that something might endure and remain, and so as a practice of lifelong orders is suited to this metaphor. But the passage also conveys the anxiety of impermanence, against the threat of which salt is required. Salt, we are warned, may end up in futility and uselessness. Does this undo the appropriateness of indelibility? By no means, for there is nothing in ourselves that holds the power to endure. The One who remains to eternity is the one who utters the Sermon on the Mount, as well as the promises for which the lifelong priest is a sign and a steward. We are at once "justified" by His promise, and in ourselves sinners. So at one and the same time we are able

28. One thinks of Stanley Hauerwas with his "resident aliens," Hans Frei with his distinct narrative, and George Lindbeck with his distinct Christian grammar, along with a host of younger scholars in their wake.

to be signs of Christ's enduring promises as He wishes, and yet are quite liable to be trodden under foot.

Finally, we have admitted that the priest in this generation will continue to suffer stress and discouragement. Theological arguments do not, as we have admitted, take such stresses away. It turns out, however, that what priests really lack is a clear sense of the meaning of their own office. Theological arguments can throw us back on the words of Scripture, "you are the salt of the earth." These words of the Lord, bestowing our identity, first as children of God, then as signs for the sake of our fellow children, do give us the "one thing needful."

Bibliography

Aquinas, Thomas. *The Summa Theologica of St. Thomas Aquinas*. 5 vols. New York: Benziger, 1948.

Anglican/Roman Catholic International Commission. *The Gift of Authority: Authority in the Church III*. Toronto: Anglican Book Centre, 1999.

Augustine. *Confessions*. Translated by F. J. Sheed. 2d ed., with notes by Michael P. Foley. Indianapolis: Hackett, 2006.

Bonhoeffer, Dietrich. *Letters and Papers from Prison*. Edited by Eberhard Bethge. New York: Macmillan, 1972.

Borgeson, Jospehine, and Lynne Wilson, editors. *Reshaping Ministry: Essays in Memory of Wesley Frensdorff*. Arvada: Jethro, 1990.

Campenhausen, Hans Freiherr von. *Ecclesiastical Authority and Spiritual Power in the Churches of the First Three Centuries*. Peabody, MA: Hendrickson, 1997.

Carter, Grayson. *Anglican Evangelicals: Protestant Secessions from the Via Media, c. 1800–1850*. Oxford: Oxford University Press, 2001.

Cox, David. *Priesthood in a New Millennium: Toward an Understanding of Anglican Presbyterate in the Twenty-First Century*. New York: Church Publishing, 2004.

Countryman, L. William. *The Language of Ordination: Ministry in an Ecumenical Context*. Philadelphia: Trinity, 1992.

De Pree, Max. *Leadership Jazz*. New York: Dell, 2993.

Farrer, Austin. *The Glass of Vision*. London: Dacre, 1948.

Gibaut, John St. H. *The Cursus Honororum: A Study of Origins and Evolution of Sequential Ordiantion*. Patristics Studies 3. New York: Lang, 2000.

Greenleaf, Robert K. *The Servant as Leader*. Indianapolis: Greenleaf, 1991.

Guthrie, Clifton. "Sacral Power: A De-Centered Theology of Clergy Authority." PhD dissertation, Emory University, 1996.

Hands, Donald R., and Wayne L. Fehr. *Spiritual Wholeness for Clergy: A New Psychology of Intimacy with God, Self, and Others*. New York: Alban Institute, 1993.

Hatchett, Marion J. *Sanctifying Life, Time, and Space: An Introduction to Liturgical Study*. New York: Seabury, 1976.

Harding, Leander. "What Have We Been Telling Ourselves About Priesthood?" *Sewanee Theological Review* 43:2 (2000) 199–206.

———. "The Power and Dignity of the Priesthood." In *Sewanee Theological Review* 43:2 (2000) 200–201.

Hummel, Charles E. *The Fire In The Fireplace: Contemporary Charismatic Renewal*. Downers Grove, IL: InterVarsity, 1980.

Hybels, Bill. *Courageous Leadership*. Grand Rapids: Zondervan, 2002.

Keck, David. *Forgetting Whose We Are: Alzheimer's Disease and the Love of God*. Nashville: Abingdon, 1996.

Luther, Martin. "The Heidelberg Disputation." In *Martin Luther's Basic Theological Writings*, edited by Timothy F. Lull, 30–49. Minneapolis: Fortress, 1989.

Macintyre, Alasdair. *After Virtue: A Study in Moral Theory*. 2d ed. Notre Dame: University of Notre Dame Press, 1984.

Mead, Loren. *The Once and Future Church: Reinventing the Congregation for a New Mission Frontier*. Washington DC: Alban Institute, 1991.

Moberly, Robert Campbell. *Ministerial Priesthood: Chapters (Preliminary to the Study of the Ordinal) on the Rationale and Meaning of Christian Priesthood*. 2d ed. Reprinted with a new introduction by A. T. Hanson. London: SPCK, 1969.

On Leadership. Harvard Business Review Paperback Series. Boston: Harvard Business School Press, 1998.

Oswald, Roy M. *Clergy Self-Care: Finding a Balance for Effective Ministry*. Washington DC: Alban Institute, 1991.

Pannenberg, Wolfhart. *The Church*. Translated by Keith Crim. Philadelphia: Westminster, 1983.

Perri, William. *A Radical Challenge for Priesthood Today: From Trial to Transformation*. Mystic, CT: Twenty-third Publications, 1996.

Peterson, Eugene H., and Marva J. Dawn. *The Unnecessary Pastor: Rediscovering the Call*. Edited by Peter Santucci. Grand Rapids: Eerdmans, 2000.

Radner, Ephraim. *The End of the Church: A Pneumatology of Christian Division in the West*. Grand Rapids: Eerdmans, 1998.

———. *Hope Among the Fragments*. Grand Rapids: Brazos, 2004.

Radner, Ephraim, and Russell R. Reno, eds. *Inhabiting Unity: Theological Perspectives on the Proposed Lutheran-Episcopal Concordat*. Grand Rapids: Eerdmans, 1995.

Rahner, Karl. *Foundations of Christian Faith: An Introduction to the Idea of Christianity*. Translated by William V. Dych. New York: Seabury, 1978.

Ramsey, Michael. *The Gospel and the Catholic Church*. London: SPCK, 1990.

Rediger, G. Lloyd. *Coping With Clergy Burnout*. Valley Forge, PA: Judson, 1982.

Seitz, Christopher. Unpublished conference paper delivered at Scholarly Engagement with Anglican Doctrine Conference in Dallas, Texas, in March, 2002.

Sumner, George. "Inaugural Address." *Toronto Journal of Theology* 15:2 (1999) 199–204.

Sykes, Stephen. "The Apostolicity of Bishop and People as a Sign of the Kingdom of God." In *Inhabiting Unity*, edited by Ephraim Radner and Russell R. Reno, 19–31. Grand Rapids: Eerdmans, 1995.

Taylor, John V. *The Growth of the Church in Buganda: An Attempt at Understanding*. London: SCM, 1958.

Terwilliger, Robert E., and Urban T. Holmes, editors. *To Be A Priest: Perspectives on Vocation and Ordination*. New York: Seabury, 1975.

Thorton, Martin. *Pastoral Theology: A Reorientation*. London: SPCK, 1956.

Torrance, Thomas F. *Royal Priesthood: A Theology of Ordained Ministry*. Edinburgh: T. & T. Clark, 1983.

Turner. Victor. *The Ritual Process: Structure and Anti-structure.* The Lewis and Henry Morgan Lectures. New York: Aldine de Gruyter, 1995.

Warren, Max Alexander Cunningham. *Revival, An Enquiry.* London: SCM, 1954.

Webster, John. *Word and Church: Essays in Church Dogmatics.* Edinburgh: T. & T. Clark, 2001.

Weems, Lovett H. *Church Leadership: Vision, Team, Culture, Integrity.* Nashville: Abingdon, 1993.

Williams, Rowan. "Imagining the Kingdom: Some Questions for Anglican Worship Today." In *The Identity of Anglican Worship,* edited by K. Stevenson and B. Spinks, 1–13. Harrisburg, PA: Morehouse, 1991.

Willimon, William H. *Clergy and Laity Burnout.* Creative Leadership Series. Nashville: Abingdon, 1989.

World Council of Churches. *Baptism, Eucharist, and Ministry.* Faith and Order Paper 111. Geneva: WCC, 1982.

Wright, Robert. "The Origins of the Episcopate and Episcopal Ministry in the Early Church." In *On Being a Bishop,* edited by Robert Wright, 13–14. New York: Church Pension Fund, 1993.

Zahl, Paul. *A Short Systematic Theology.* Grand Rapids: Eerdmans, 2000.

Scripture Index

OLD TESTAMENT

Exodus

19:6, 6

Psalms

23:6, 57

Song of Songs

8:6, 52

Jeremiah

32:9–15, 98

NEW TESTAMENT

Matthew

5:13, 100
28:16–20, 33
28:20, 52, 84

Mark

10:2–9, 52

John

1:39, 57
10:1–18, 54
13:1, 52

Acts

20:28, 7

Romans

12:1, 24

1 Corinthians

1:26, 47
4:16, 47
7:32, 47
12:3, 66
15:3–11, 33

Ephesians

4:1–12, 33
4:1–4, 55
4:11, 7
5:31–33, 52
5:32, 47, 52

Colossians

1:17, 55
1:19, 57
4:6, 100

1 Timothy

3:1–7, 51
3:2, 52, 53
3:5, 52
3:9, 51

Hebrews

4, 57
13:8, 84

1 Peter

2:5, 6
5:2–4, 7

1 John

1:1–3, 33

Revelation

20, 57